URBAN
eco
CHIC

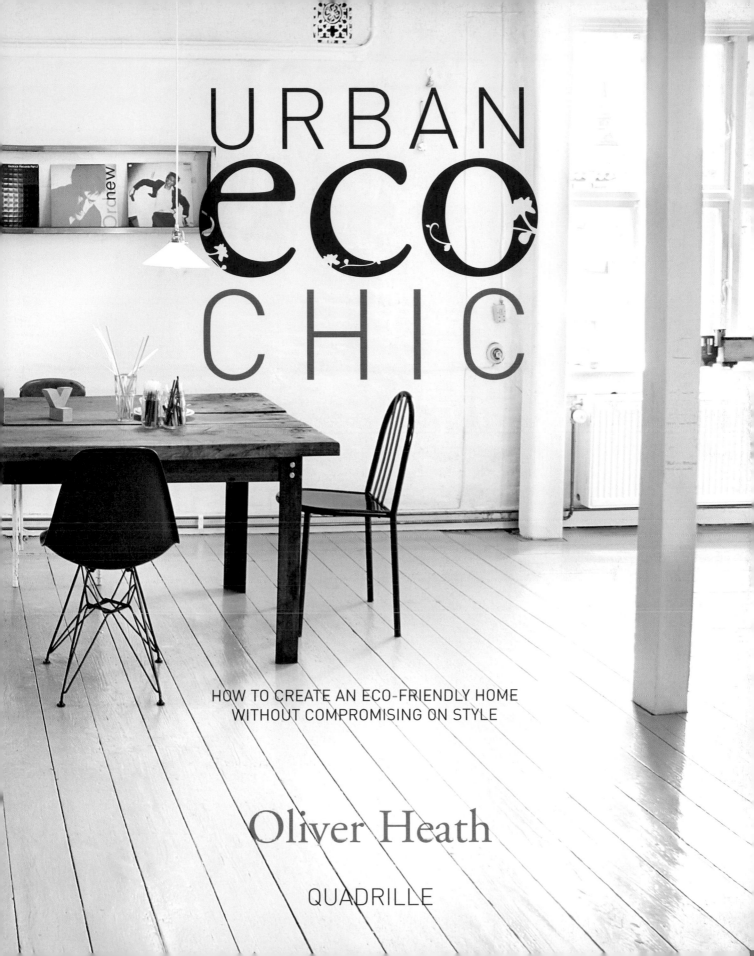

URBAN
eco
CHIC

HOW TO CREATE AN ECO-FRIENDLY HOME
WITHOUT COMPROMISING ON STYLE

Oliver Heath

QUADRILLE

For my girls, Katie, Lyla and Chick Pea.
For whom a beautiful and sustainable future is so worthwhile.

This book is printed in the European Community by Grafos S.A. in Spain using vegetable-based inks. The paper for the book was produced by Artic Paper Munkedal AB in Sweden and Poland, who have full FSC accreditation for all of their papers. They operate some of the most environmentally friendly paper mills in the world, combining the latest technology with a practice of sustainable forest and land management that conserves biodiversity, soil, and water resources, and safeguards the health and ecology of ecosystems. The jacket for this book is printed on FSC accredited paper and coated with a matt lamination that is fully recyclable.

Mixed Sources
Product group from well-managed
forests and other controlled sources
www.fsc.org   Cert no.   SGS-COC-2086
© 1996 Forest Stewardship Council
FSC

Editorial Director Jane O'Shea
Creative Director Helen Lewis
Designer Claire Peters
Project Editor Lisa Pendreigh
Picture Researcher Helen Stallion
Production Director Vincent Smith
Production Controller Ruth Deary

First published in 2008 by
Quadrille Publishing

ISBN: 978 184400 644 1

Printed in Spain

Library of Congress Cataloging-in-Publication Data

Heath, Oliver.
  Urban eco chic : how to live in an eco-friendly way without compromising
on style / Oliver Heath.
    p. cm.
  Includes index.
  ISBN 978-1-84400-644-1 (hardback)
  1. Interior decoration--Environmental aspects. 2. Architecture,
Domestic--Environmental aspects. I. Title.
  NK2113.H43 2008
  747--dc22

                                    2008027768

As an interior designer, I feel a responsibility to do all I can to highlight the issue of climate change and the effect it is having on our lives and homes. The world we inhabit is changing due to our activities, and as it changes we must adapt our lifestyles to compensate. I am not interested in relaying messages of doom and destruction, nor do I wish to layer on guilt to shame people into changing their ways. I prefer to take on board the facts of climate change and embrace a way of living that reduces my impact on the environment, but at the same time allows my home to be stylish and comfortable. After all, I am a designer who wants things to be just so—for form, function, and sustainability go hand in hand in hand.

My passion for eco-design comes from a number of threads. A childhood spent playing on Brighton beach and in Sussex woodlands, in England, led to a fascination with nature. But it was when I became a windsurfing instructor aged 18 that I learned to respect nature. Teaching others about the dangers we face when we take nature's power for granted gave me more experience—and scars—than I ever intended. We humans often forget how we are part of the natural world rather than set apart from it. Studying architecture for six years allowed me to combine my passion for nature with the built environment, exploring how our homes can work in tandem with nature, rather than against it.

Working in interior design, I am committed to finding ways of reducing our eco-impact without compromising on style—to create a home that benefits both us and the environment. When I say "benefits" us, I mean it will cost less to run, be more comfortable to live in, contain fewer toxins, and be a nurturing, comforting, inspiring place to call home. My aim is to make sustainable interiors accessible yet aspirational, without being overly expensive.

Over a number of years, I have accumulated my ideas on eco-design, and this book has provided an exciting opportunity to gather them together. My television design work offers invaluable experience in creating homes that reflect the character of the owners. My writing work for *Friends of the*

Earth and *the Observer*, and role as spokesperson for environmental groups such as the Energy Savings Trust, affords the opportunity to research sustainable practices and materials, while private commissions for a variety of environmental groups, such as Bio Regional, offer the chance to put my eco-designs into practice.

Most important—and closest to my heart—is my own eco-home. On moving into a mid-nineteenth-century townhouse, I seized the opportunity to carry out a largely sustainable refurbishment; my goal was to create a beautiful, inspiring home with minimal environmental impact. Since my daughter Lyla was born, my efforts to reduce the level of toxins in our home have been more than justified. How could I live with myself knowing that I had unnecessarily exposed her to a toxic space? Furthermore, it is good to know that the home she lives in now has gone as far as possible in reducing any negative impact on the environment that will one day be her responsibility. Having a child has really put all these messages into a very clear perspective for me.

In 2005, with my business partner Nikki Blustin, I set up EcoCentric—an online store for well designed, environmentally conscious homewares. Excited by the diverse culture of sustainability springing up, I wanted to make these products available to a wider design-conscious audience who were turned off by unattractive, functional eco-products. EcoCentric has given me a real understanding of the issues surrounding homewares and the impact these seemingly innocuous products have both in the home and upon the environment.

My philosophy of urban eco-chic is in some way a reaction to the cheap throwaway consumer society in which we currently find ourselves, where homes appear devoid of authenticity and quality. Too many of the homes I visit are filled with anonymous, low-quality flat-pack furniture, where personal expression is traded in for quick, cheap fixes of accessible furniture and nightmarish shopping experiences. Instead, what we need is good, durable design that is multifunctional, easily repaired, and manufactured responsibly. I truly believe that we all need to rethink the fundamental criteria of what we term "contemporary design." After all, if current design practice does not take into account one of society's major issues, what relevance does it really have to the contemporary needs of our homes, lives and planet?

In an era of eco-guilt, worries over debt, fears of terrorism, and high levels of work stress, there is a need to create feel-good homes—a space that is as good to live in as it is for the environment. It is far more relaxing to sit back at the end of the day in the knowledge that your home is doing its part (and saving you money, too). Our homes are a model for the way in which we treat the planet: they are the universe in microcosm. In its truest sense, eco-design is about living with as small an environmental footprint as possible—living in smaller homes, using fewer products and resources—a minimalist way of living. However, this is not always possible, and so I want to help you find a realistic way to embrace the benefits of eco-design through urban eco-chic.

For most of us, living in a new, purpose-built eco-house will remain an unachievable dream. Where I live, in Britain, 98% of the housing stock is existing period property; and much of it is creaky, leaky, and drafty. But do not let that deter you from going eco, as there is so much you can do to make where you already live better, whether it is an apartment or a house. After all, you will be adapting what is already existing, and so will neither have to produce nor demolish anything. You are just going to make it better and better; now that is a positive thing to do.

I have written this book not with specific examples or brands given but with key information and general suggestions to be investigated further, ideally locally or via the Internet. I believe that the eco-movement is the most significant development of recent times. It is something we must embrace and work with, seizing the opportunities that it offers. I hope this book opens you up to some of the amazing possibilities that face our homes, and lives, both now and in the future.

ABOVE An elegant expression of
urban eco-chic. The light-reflective
white walls and floors of this
beautifully proportioned living room
provide the perfect backdrop for a
collection of vintage furniture,
including a sofa reupholstered in
colorful patchwork and a mid-20th-
century Italian standard lamp.

PRINCIPLES

WHY ECO?

IT WAS ARCHITECT
ELIEL SAARINEN WHO SAID,
IN 1956, "ALWAYS DESIGN A
THING BY CONSIDERING IT IN
ITS NEXT LARGER CONTEXT—
A CHAIR IN A ROOM, A ROOM
IN A HOUSE, A HOUSE IN AN
ENVIRONMENT, AN
ENVIRONMENT IN A
CITY PLAN."

Now, more than ever before, this maxim is applicable to our age—when we must consider everything we design, buy, and use in our homes in a wider context. Although this quote predates the current era of eco-consciousness, the concept rings truer now than it did in the 1950s—it puts our homes into the context of their surrounding communities and reminds us that in scale, small changes in how we live really can make a big difference.

From a technological point of view, our homes are now under ever-closer scrutiny to use less energy, to output less waste, and so to become more efficient in their use of the world's resources. That is not surprising when we consider that the average home produces 6.6 tons of carbon dioxide (CO_2) emissions every year. The CO_2 produced by each home is a "greenhouse gas," which contributes to global warming and so directly accelerates climate change. If some simple principles were applied to tackling the amount of domestic CO_2 emissions, that figure could easily be reduced by one-third—yes, that is more than 2 tons less per household. Not only will this lessen the impact that each home has on the environment; it will also save us all money into the bargain.

ABOVE This spacious open-plan kitchen and dining area incorporates a bank of sleek, pale plywood units with integral appliances, however the space is saved from appearing sterile by the addition of a gently worn farmhouse table and assortment of vintage metal chairs, crowned by a glamorous ornate chandelier.

So if both the message and the motive are clear, why are we not all doing more? There is a misconception that we can live in a more environmentally sustainable way only if we abandon our existing homes to move into shiny new grass-roofed, turbine-powered eco-houses; that our old energy-inefficient homes are as leaky as sieves, so why bother improving them?

Well, the reality is that living in a more sustainable way need not entail moving; but you may well need to spend a little money on doing a little maintenance work in order to make your home fit for the twenty-first century. This century looks set to show us that if the existing unsustainable levels of domestic CO_2 emissions continue, it is our own habitable environment we are in danger of destroying, rather than the planet itself. But the problem is, Where to start?

WHAT IS ECO-DESIGN?

Traditionally, good design for the home has been about bringing together a number of different aspects to create the ideal living space; Location, function, style, and cost all have to be balanced (with a touch of inspiration, of course) within the perfect home. However, a new and pressing issue has landed upon our doorsteps, adding another aspect to designing a home, one that urgently must be considered alongside the rest. Current environmental concerns dictate that our homes must go beyond our personal comfort to become more conscious of the wider needs of the planet. We must consider the impact our homes are having on the environment and how we can all lessen the detrimental effect our choices in life are wreaking on the planet.

In the past, eco-design was considered to be the preserve of people generally considered to be tree-hugging hippies; but their ideas are now acknowledged as becoming ever more relevant within today's society. The eco-hippy approach to design could be summed up as "less is more"—a philosophy that encouraged followers to tread lightly upon the earth.

Some sectors of society were quick to ridicule this ideal—a functional bare aesthetic intertwined with an alternative spiritual belief system—largely as it presented a rejection of the conventional notions of Western consumerism. But spiritual values aside, from a practical perspective there are many lessons that we can learn from this "alternative" way of living.

REDUCE, REUSE, RECYCLE

Eco-design's fundamental lifestyle "mantra" (okay, I know that word does sound a little hippy-ish, but stick with it) is known as the 3 Rs, that is:
REDUCE ⦿ **REUSE** ⦿ **RECYCLE**

REDUCE is about reducing your consumption of resources—whether it be the basic utilities that feed your home, such as gas, water, and electricity, or more general consumable goods, such as furniture, clothing, packaging, and foodstuffs. Being realistic, it does not mean living a frugal, minimalist life but, rather, a more efficient and thoughtful one.

REUSE refers to the sustainable methods by which the products we consume are made. They should come from well-managed sources that are naturally replenished. This includes materials such as wood, wool, cork, and rubber. "Reuse" can also refer to products that have been reappropriated; this can be as simple as a chair given a new lease on life with a lick of paint or an armchair revived by new upholstery. In addition, it includes other items, from fabrics to foods, that hail from a fair-trade and/or organic source; products that in the process of their manufacture have not unnecessarily depleted or damaged the earth's resources or put others' lives in misery, starvation, or poverty.

RECYCLE differs from "reuse" in that it refers to materials that are totally broken down—used cardboard, glass, and paper—and then reassembled in another form to create new products. Recycling ensures that materials are not taken out of their useful lifecycle loop only to be cast into landfill or incinerated. Our planet does not possess limitless supplies of raw materials, so it is essential that we make the most of what we have. It is now possible to recycle nearly 70% of what goes into our homes—glass, tin, paper, plastics, clothes and fabrics, paints—in fact, almost everything can go somewhere if you simply take the time to think about it.

The 3 Rs sit in a logical hierarchy. Foremost it is better to consume less. So, to begin with, **REDUCE**—be efficient with what you use, and do not take anything for granted. If you really cannot use less, make sure that what you do consume comes from a well-managed, renewable, sustainable source—in other words **REUSE**. Lastly, make certain that what you do consume does not end up in landfill or incinerated. Prolong the active life cycle of materials by allowing them to be reused in another form—so **RECYCLE**. Recycling is at the bottom of the 3Rs eco-hierarchy, because it takes energy to collect materials, chop them up, and then re-form them into new products. Nevertheless recycling plays a vital role in achieving a sustainable world and lifestyle.

> IT IS BETTER TO CONSUME LESS. SO, TO BEGIN WITH, REDUCE—BE EFFICIENT WITH WHAT YOU USE, AND DO NOT TAKE ANYTHING FOR GRANTED.

OPPOSITE This pared-down dining room has a relaxed, unfussy feel. The light-colored walls keep it fresh and airy—reducing the need for additional artificial light. The use of natural materials, including the wooden plank tabletop, offers a simplicity and earthiness, while the mismatched vintage chairs add character and stop the space from feeling too precious.

A well-designed eco-home incorporates key features based around the 3-Rs mantra. The emphasis within any eco-home is to reduce the amount of resources it consumes by making the most of the site that it sits on and incorporating the following features within the build:

- glazing on the building's south side to take in warmth from the sun
- minimal openings on the building's north side to reduce heat loss
- sun-shading louvers or plantation shutters to reduce the amount of summer sun entering the building but allow the lower winter sun in
- renewable energy sources, such as solar water heating, photovoltaic panels, or a wind turbine secured to the walls or roof
- heavily insulated roofs, walls, and ground floors
- a solid section made from brick, concrete, or stone that acts as a heat sink to store the sun's energy (known as thermal mass)
- double glazing or storm windows
- an extremely efficient heating system
- a minimal number of (low-energy) electrical light fittings
- appliances, such as fridges and freezers, with the Energy Star rating
- reduced-flow water systems, such as low-flow faucets and showers, dual-flush toilets, and gray water storage systems

An eco-home can be constructed with sustainable materials, including:
- a wood construction with wooden siding and fittings, such as doors, window frames, and banisters;
- sheep's-wool insulation;
- natural flooring materials, such as wood, wool, or cork;
- nontoxic natural paints;
- green turfed roof, which insulates and encourages local biodiversity.

An efficient eco-home will reflect an awareness of which resources can be recycled and make the most of them in these ways:
- a gray (used) water recycling system
- heat pumps to recycle surplus warm air
- recyclable materials, such as stainless steel and wood surfaces
- recycling bins in the kitchen and a compost pile in the garden

ECO-DESIGN VERSUS ECO-CHIC

While the 3-Rs mantra, which lies at the very heart of eco- design, appears rather basic, this apparent simplicity belies its complex nature when applied in its strictest form. Within the creation of an environmentally friendly home, staying true to core eco-design principles presents some fascinating challenges. An eco-house is a utilitarian piece of design in which functional efficiency is placed above all else; any nod toward style is considered a bonus. After all, in the face of such an enormous issue as global warming and the destruction of our habitat, why would we consider trivialities such as style to be important?

The creation of eco-efficient homes is a noble aim for architects and designers to strive toward. The world of design is courageously doing battle with the wastefulness of society; but—and this is a big but—there is a fundamental problem with architectural efficiency and the nature of human beings. We are emotional creatures; we have passions, likes, and dislikes, and, just occasionally, we are a little irrational. We are guided by our instincts and act upon emotional responses. For many the spare minimalism that accompanies the ultra-efficiency of pure eco-design can be a real turnoff; our personal needs are often more complex than its minimalist specifications allow.

Eco-design has provided the architectural theory and technological know how by which to design the energy-efficient House of the Future, but I question whether it will help you to create the perfect Home of the Future. When creating a home, I want color, atmosphere, personality, and soul—and I, for one, am not prepared to give these things up readily.

Here I see a dichotomy between the asceticism eco-purists dictate we need to live by in order to be green and the emotionalism inherent in all of us that fuels our personal desire for comfort. Acting as a bridge between the extreme eco-minimalism espoused by activists and the universal human need to create a nurturing space, eco-chic offers a sustainable way of living that is at once comfortable and enticing. Eco-chic is a decorating style that follows the concepts of eco-design yet does not expect you to forgo the level of style that we have all come to demand within our homes.

ECO-CHIC OFFERS A SUSTAINABLE WAY OF LIVING THAT IS AT THE SAME TIME COMFORTABLE AND ENTICING.

Sustainable living is all about community; after all, what is the point in only one house within a city being environmentally conscious. A community offers us all the opportunity to work together, to share resources, and to make financial savings. If eco-design in its purest form does not excite and inspire the masses, it will be taken up by only a minority. With ambitious quotas in the reduction of carbon emissions being set, such limited appeal is a huge problem. Eco-chic, however, allows us to create energy-efficient homes that are beautifully designed and really stimulate and excite us by appealing to our emotional sides.

URBAN ECO-CHIC

The society we live in is a highly visual one, with style messages constantly being played out on the television and within the media. As a result, style plays a key role in our personal expression—it is an essential outlet for the way that we present ourselves to the world—announcing what we like and dislike, our experiences, preferences, and our social grouping. A world without style is practically unimaginable. Can you envisage a world where you lived in a sterile white box and dressed in the same way every day—and, worse still, where everyone around you did the same?

Although the dilemma of deciding what to wear each day would be a thing of the past, there would be no self-expression or individuality. Instead, it would be a soulless and anonymous existence. Clearly, design has a key role to play in so many aspects of our lives that we cannot be expected to just drop it when designing our homes. I believe that good design can actually help us to embrace essential trends, and in that way make the pure functionality of eco-design a sweeter, more aspirational choice. Okay, so it might be a little more challenging to go green, but that is exactly why we have to exercise a little creativity in this problem solving.

In my emotionally led designer's mind, style always comes first. Good design seduces you; it compels you to respond emotionally; in short, it will make you fall in love with a product or a space. Tapping into this emotional response is essential if a movement such as eco-design is to be embraced universally.

Urban eco-chic is about creating a balance between style and function, with a conscious effort to reduce one's environmental impact. It is a thoughtful style that considers the wider impact of design on the environment in which it exists. It is now impossible to discuss modern design without sustainability being a key part of that debate. Good design must be beautiful, functional, and now inherently green.

The performance of each product we use is now critical. It is a subject that we are all familiar with when discussing cars: we would not contemplate buying a car without first asking how many miles to the gallon it does, how fast is it 0 to 60 mph, or how many seats it has. But only now are we starting to realize that performance (as boring a concept as it may seem) also relates to our homes. Performance is not solely about energy efficiency; it is also about the use of space, storage, and multifunctional adaptability.

Urban eco-chic brings together the demands of performance with the style-led aspects of contemporary living. It is a pioneering style, one for a new age of social and environmental development, a style to embrace as a community—one that benefits us all and generations to come. When you start to see the bigger picture of what a style movement can really do, it becomes even more exciting.

OPPOSITE This bedroom uses recycled floorboards to stunning effect on a feature wall, bringing texture to the space and creating a wonderful visual contrast with the luxurious draperies. Organic fair-trade bed linens encourage a sound night's sleep in a toxin-free environment, enhanced by the knowledge that it is ethically produced. Hardwood flooring, teamed with just a small bedside rug, helps to keep the space dust- and allergen-free.

KEY ECO-QUESTIONS TO ASK OF EVERY MATERIAL AND PRODUCT

Where has it come from?
● Is it from a naturally renewable source?
● Was it made in a nonpolluting, energy-efficient way?
● Were the rights of the workers respected with good conditions, reasonable hours, and fair pay?
● Will it travel vast distances to reach me? Can I choose a locally made product instead?

How will I use it?
● Will it be energy efficient, saving me money and saving the environment carbon emissions?
● Is it built to last, or will it fall apart as soon as the guarantee ends?
● Is it easy to maintain and fix? Am I able to get spare parts easily?

Where will it go once I am done with it?
● Can I pass it on to someone else to use after I have finished with it?
● Can I recycle it easily?
● Will it biodegrade?

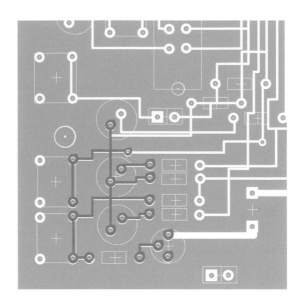

ASPECTS OF URBAN ECO CHIC

THERE ARE THREE ESSENTIAL ASPECTS OF URBAN ECO-CHIC THAT NEED TO BE CONSIDERED IN ORDER TO INCORPORATE THE FUNCTIONALITY OF ECO DESIGN AND THE 3 R'S INTO A STYLE THAT IS AS GOOD TO LIVE WITH AS IT IS FOR THE ENVIRONMENT.

TECHNOLOGY

Technology is the key to how we can reduce our environmental impact and lower our carbon emissions. It is an exciting area, which is constantly developing. Modern technology is becoming smaller, better, faster, and (most importantly) more efficient. Embracing all that technology has to offer will allow us to make our lives less wasteful and more efficient and to harness more of what occurs naturally around us—such as renewable energies from the sun, wind, earth, and sea.

We must trust that developments in technology will help us to reduce our impact on the environment and to combat climate change. Technology refers to methods of creating renewable energy, super-insulating materials, and ultra-efficient appliances, but also to cutting-edge materials, be they new low-impact materials, natural, or even recycled.

NATURE

Nature is an essential component of our lives that we sometimes take for granted. Interaction with nature is a grounding force; it quite literally brings us back down to earth and reminds us that we are part of the natural world. The vibrant scent of freshly mown grass, the textural feel of tree bark, the flickering flames of a log fire—these all raise simple but primeval emotional responses within us, which are essentially comforting. Natural materials often improve with age and use, developing a unique character, adding individuality and a certain richness to any home.

The use of natural materials not only brings textural sensuousness to the home but also allows us to choose sustainable and naturally renewable materials—materials that, when responsibly managed, have a lower impact on the environment. If chosen and finished carefully, nature will allow you to reduce the number of man-made toxins in your home, creating a healthier space to live in.

VINTAGE

I am using "vintage" as an umbrella term that opens us up to the glamour of antiques, the ingenuity of reuse, and even the excitement of flea-market finds. It is about making the most of what we already have produced and finding new ways of using things—offering a new lease on life for a discarded item. The pleasure of vintage is all about invention—putting a new spin on an existing object—be that through repositioning, framing, grouping, or remaking.

But more than finding new ways of using old things, it is about harnessing the sense of style inherent within the object. Vintage items may add a touch of glamour to our lives, which is always a good thing. Furthermore, vintage items can have a softening quality; that wear and tear simply cannot be reproduced, so vintage pieces have the effect of taking the harder edge off a contemporary interior. This patina of age speaks of experience and uniqueness that money just cannot buy in this age of mass production.

The three aspects of urban eco-chic can be interpreted in a number of ways and can help solve style and functional dilemmas when trying to create your own eco-home. What we will discover is that certain rooms of the home naturally show a bias toward one of these three aspects over the other two, due to their function and status as a public/private space or as one that uses more or fewer resources.

● Kitchens have a heavier slant toward technology, as this is an area where many resources (gas, water, electricity) are used, and so it needs to be as efficient as possible.
🍂 Kitchens may also lean toward nature for some materials, which may align with our tastes for natural and organic foods.
🍂 Bathrooms may have a heavier slant to nature, as this is a sensual space, so using natural materials to create a spa-like feel will be very relaxing, while technology will help us to reduce our use of resources.
❀ Bedrooms, being private spaces, may have a greater leaning toward the vintage, which carries romantic, nostalgic associations, while nature will lend a sense of simplicity and purity.
🍂 ❀ ● Living rooms may well lean toward nature, vintage, and then technology, being public spaces—thus reflecting a variety of your interests and activities, such as books, music, ornaments, photographs, music, or film.

In this way urban eco-chic is open to a certain amount of personal interpretation; it is a flexible style through which you can express your own tastes and experiences while sustaining your passion for a cleaner, greener way of living.

ABOVE This living room favors the nature and vintage aspects of urban eco-chic to create a relaxed yet personal space, which speaks volumes about the owners.

Sometimes the technological elements of a room can
remain hidden; radiant, infloor, heating keeps this space
cozy with no visible heat source.

RESOURCES

ECO-CONSCIENCE

IT IS IMPORTANT TO REMEMBER THAT URBAN ECO-CHIC IS A STYLE WITH A CONSCIENCE. IT IS MORE THAN JUST THIS SEASON'S COLOR; IT IS, RATHER, A WAY OF LIFE. UNUSUALLY, IT IS ONE THAT BALANCES STYLISTIC CHOICES WITH TECHNICAL PERFORMANCE TO PRODUCE INTERIORS THAT ARE AS GOOD TO LIVE WITH AS THEY ARE FOR THE ENVIRONMENT.

It is important to consider the bigger picture of the ways in which we live and to get out of the short-term view that saving small amounts of money now is our primary objective. I feel that it is better to consider the possible greater long-term gains and to take a level of social responsibility for our actions.

Like many parents, I was compelled by the birth of my daughter to think hard about our environmental future and whether I was personally doing as much as I could toward securing a safe habitat for our future generations. If we do not take action against climate change now, our own children will face an even greater threat. Much of the campaigning around environmental issues is designed to tug on our guilty heartstrings. But although our foe—the notorious carbon emissions—is invisible, it is clear that we all must act fast.

For a long time, guilt has been a key ally in the battle to convert people to a more sustainable way of living, but I believe it need not be that way. There is a direct necessity for a change in attitude toward adopting eco-friendly measures within our homes, but we could be doing it through positive free will and

OPPOSITE With urban eco-chic there is no compromise when it comes to style—it is about creating a home that is as good to live with as it is for the environment. In my own home, form, function, and environmental concerns work together to create a space that is as luxurious as it is healthful.

aspiration, rather than through negative guilt. Even something as seemingly mundane as an eco-efficient home can be an exciting challenge if looked upon with vision—not to mention the fact that with energy prices on the rise, our homes are becoming ever more expensive to run. So the possible saving in fuel costs could be a clear incentive to take action. We could be actively embracing change. After all, there are so many positive benefits to be had—not least, the amount of money to be saved. More than that, there is the legacy we will leave behind for our children and grandchildren through reducing the impact that our homes are needlessly having on the environment.

WHAT IS A CARBON FOOTPRINT?

You cannot fail to have noticed all the recent talk of carbon. Just a few years ago, the only carbon we all worried about was the stuff we scraped off our burned toast! However, the word "carbon" has crept up on us and is now one of society's burning issues (if you will excuse the pun).

When discussing a carbon footprint, what we are really referring to is carbon dioxide (CO_2) emissions. In a nutshell, CO_2 is produced every time we make or burn something, and so virtually every action we take contributes to our carbon footprint. The real problem occurs when we excavate fossil fuels—coal, oil, and gas—which for millions of years have been buried under the earth, and introduce them into our environment. When these resources are burned they produce energy, some of which we use, some of which is lost, and some of which becomes CO_2.

CO_2 is one of the "greenhouse gases"; and much as their name suggests, these gases have a warming effect on our environment. Energy from the sun is mainly absorbed by the earth's surface, but around 30% of this energy is reflected back into the atmosphere in infrared wavelengths. The increasing presence of CO_2 and other greenhouse gases in the earth's atmosphere since industrialization has resulted in more of this infrared energy being trapped within the earth's lower atmosphere, rather than escaping into space. Once trapped, it causes a further warming of the atmosphere, known as the "greenhouse effect." This process has led to global warming, wreaking all sorts of damage upon the balance of our environment.

The problem with CO_2 is that the damn stuff is invisible. So just how do we start to take with due seriousness something we cannot physically see? And concerning ourselves with our own carbon footprint is all very well, but why should we be individually responsible if it is really heavy industry and distant power plants that are churning out all this CO_2?

The truth is that almost every action we take—however trivial—has an impact on the environment; even the simple act of switching on a light sends a message to the power plant to burn more fuel and produce more CO_2. If we add up the CO_2 emissions associated with all those individual actions, it produces what is termed a carbon footprint. Simply put, a carbon footprint is a measure in units (or tons) of CO_2 of how your life's activities impact on the environment in terms of the greenhouse gases produced.

There are two aspects to your carbon footprint:
• A primary footprint is produced as a direct result of your day-to-day activities, such as your use of gas, electricity, and water in the home and through car journeys.
• A secondary footprint is created through the indirect choices that you make and reflect the CO_2 produced by the whole life cycle of the products you choose. For example, you buy a plastic hairdryer made in China, which travels around the globe, uses lots of energy before it eventually dies, is then thrown away, and ends up in a landfill site, where it slowly decomposes over the following 200,000 years or so. Phew! This single purchase will undoubtedly have a high carbon footprint, so it is critical that you examine the life cycle of each product that you consume and consider its environmental impact.

Share of public services 12%

Financial services 3%

Recreation and leisure 14%

Household (buildings and furnishings) 9%

Car manufacture 7%

Clothes and personal effects 4%

Food and drink 5%

Vacation flights 6%

Public transportation 3%

Private transportation 10%

Electricity 12%

Gas, oil, and coal 15%

A TYPICAL CARBON FOOTPRINT

The chart above gives a basic breakdown of an average person's carbon footprint in my own country, Britain, highlighting the areas in which we create the most damage to the environment. It shows just how much work we have really got to do in the areas of our homes, recreation and leisure, and transportation.

The efficiency of our homes is becoming ever more important. Gone are the energy-rich years of the last century. We can no longer afford to be wasteful when it comes to the amount of gas and electricity we consume. Now we are living in an age when what we use and what we produce are being scrutinized—and with good

reason. Worldwide, our homes produce 19% of all greenhouse gas emissions, with the U. S. producing one-quarter of the total. The average American household produces 11.7 tons of CO_2 a year. If action were taken, with just a few simple measures, that figure could be reduced by one-third. In this way, your home reduces its impact on the environment, you create a healthier and more comfortable space to live in, and, of course, you spend less money.

When it is put like this, why wouldn't we all want to make the switch to a cleaner, greener way of living? After all, why should our homes impact unnecessarily on the environment when they really do not have to?

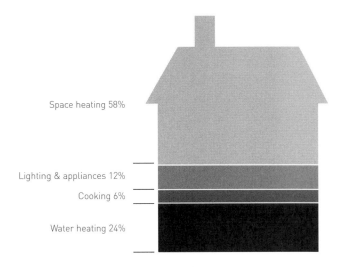

Space heating 58%

Lighting & appliances 12%

Cooking 6%

Water heating 24%

HOME RESOURCES

AN ECO-EFFICIENT HOME
MINIMIZES ITS USE OF
RESOURCES—THAT IS, GAS,
ELECTRICITY, AND WATER.
IT IS IMPORTANT TO
UNDERSTAND HOW A HOME
FUNCTIONS IN ORDER TO
IDENTIFY WHERE THE MOST
EFFECTIVE CHANGES CAN BE
MADE TO REDUCE
RESOURCES USAGE. WITH
CAREFUL PLANNING, THIS
STRICT CODE OF REDUCTION
NEED NOT LEAD TO A
COMPROMISED LIFESTYLE.

AVERAGE ENERGY USE IN THE HOME

This chart shows the proportional domestic
energy use within a typical home in a
temperate climate (with no air conditioning).
It clearly demonstrates how important the
heating of your home and water are to your
overall energy consumption (and your carbon
footprint). If you are going to focus your
energies into doing your part, your time and
money are best spent insulating your home,
and installing energy-efficient appliances,
such as Energy Star-rated furnaces and
compact fluorescent lightbulbs.

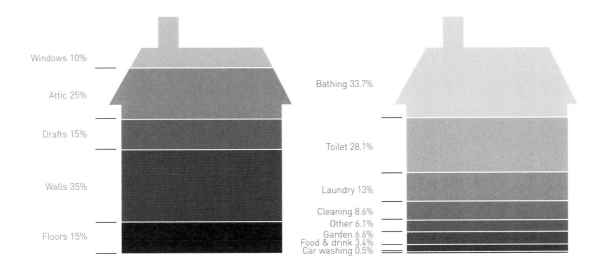

Windows 10%
Attic 25%
Drafts 15%
Walls 35%
Floors 15%

Bathing 33.7%
Toilet 28.1%
Laundry 13%
Cleaning 8.6%
Other 6.1%
Garden 6.6%
Food & drink 3.4%
Car washing 0.5%

AVERAGE HEAT LOSS IN THE HOME

The statistics shown in this chart prove that, surprisingly, more heat escapes through your walls than it does through your roof. So if you are going to spend any money, install cavity wall as well as attic insulation. Check with the I. R. S. to see if you can get a tax credit for any "green" improvements you make to your home. However, don't forget the simple things; if you can feel a draft, track down the source and fix it—the warm, heated air within your home is being cooled down by the chilly air rushing in. So your money is being wasted and the comfort of your home is being compromised.

AVERAGE WATER USE IN THE HOME

Amazingly, the water we drink and cook with accounts for only a tiny percentage of what we use, on average, at home. If you really want to cut your water usage—and bills—you should be washing with less water (for example, taking showers rather than baths if you normally take a bath—or shorter showers, if you tend to linger in them) and doing something about that wasteful toilet. Almost a third of your entire water usage is flushed away. Remember, too, that a lot of energy is spent transporting fresh water and waste water to and from consumers; in Britain, for example, these services account for 3% of the country's total energy use.

LIFESTYLE
CHANGES
LOW COST

SO HOW DO YOU START
CUTTING BACK ON THE
AMOUNT OF RESOURCES
YOU USE AT HOME? THESE
SIMPLE TIPS ARE GREAT
FOR THOSE WHO DON'T
HAVE THE CASH TO SPLASH.
IN FACT, UNLIKE SOME
GREEN MEASURES, WHICH
ENTAIL EXTRA SPENDING,
MANY OF THESE TIPS WILL
ACTUALLY SAVE YOU MONEY.

ELECTRICITY

◉ Switch to a green energy supplier, who provides power from renewable sources.
◉ Don't leave appliances on standby; turn them off. In some cases you may need to unplug them in order to disable the standby setting.
◉ Turn off the lights as you leave each room.
◉ Keep windows clean, so they let in lots of natural light; you will use less electric lighting.
◉ Position white or reflective surfaces, such as white tables and mirrors, near windows to bounce light around—it is amazingly effective. Painting walls white also helps.
◉ When boiling water for drinks, fill the kettle with only as much water as you need.
◉ Open fridge and freezer doors for as short a time as possible to prevent cool air from escaping. Keep them fully stocked, because the mass stores the coolness longer.
◉ Use a good-quality washing detergent and wash at the "warm" or "cold" setting; over a year it saves an amazing amount of energy.
◉ When possible, air-dry your washing, instead of using the drier.
◉ Cook with the lids on saucepans.
◉ Turn the lights off for an hour or two each evening and dine in romantic candlelight.
◉ Close blinds or curtains during the summer so the sun's warmth does not overheat your home.

HEATING/COOLING

◉ If you have a programmable thermostat, set it to turn the heat/air conditioning off during the hours when you're away from home and back on again 30 minutes before you are likely to return.

◉ Reduce the daytime and evening temperature on your furnace by 2°F. You are unlikely to notice the difference, and you could save up to 10% on your heating bill.

◉ Don't waste heating or air conditioning on unused rooms. Shut registers (or turn off radiators) and keep the doors closed.

◉ Fit storm windows during the winter. You can buy inexpensive interior storm windows, made of plastic film, which will do the job until you can afford better ones.

◉ Heavy draperies—lined or even interlined—will significantly cut down heat loss. They can be expensive, but you might find serviceable ones that you can alter in a secondhand store, a flea market, or even via the Internet. Some interlined Roman shades would provide good insulation at relatively little cost.

◉ On a bright winter day, open the draperies, shades, or blinds where the sun is shining to let the building soak up the warmth.

◉ If you have radiators, place shelves over them to kick the heat forward and stop it from circulating upward to the ceiling.

◉ Alternatively, fit reflective material, such as aluminum foil, behind radiators; this is amazingly effective at directing heat into the room.

WATER

◉ Get a water meter fitted; then you will be directly responsible only for the water you use.

◉ Take a shower instead of a bath; this can use just two-fifths of the 25 gallons a bath uses. A word of caution, though: standing under a normal-flow shower for more than 5 minutes could use as much water as a bath.

◉ If you are going to take a bath, share it.

◉ Do not leave the faucet running while you are brushing your teeth.

◉ Avoid unnecessary flushes of your toilet. Toilets manufactured before 1992 use between 31/2 and 7 gallons per flush (newer ones use only about 11/2 gallons per flush).

◉ If your toilet is an older model, put a displacement device in the tank to reduce the amount of water in a flush.

◉ Fix any dripping faucets.

◉ Whenever possible, wait until you have a full load of laundry or dishes before using your washer or dishwasher. Or use the half load program if available.

◉ Keep a pitcher of water cool in the fridge, instead of running the faucet until it goes cold.

◉ If you use a garden hose, fit a trigger nozzle so no water is wasted.

◉ Instead of a hose, use a bucket and sponge to wash the car the old-fashioned way.

LIFESTYLE CHANGES
MEDIUM COST

THESE ARE THE TIPS TO SAVE YOU MORE MONEY OVER A LONGER TERM. OKAY, THEY WILL COST A LITTLE CASH TO IMPLEMENT BUT IN TIME, YOU WILL REAP MUCH GREATER REWARDS THAN THE INITIAL LAYOUT. YOU MAY WANT TO CONSIDER THESE IF YOU ARE REFURBISHING YOUR HOME, DOING SOME D. I. Y. OR MOVING INTO A NEW PLACE.

ELECTRICITY

● Fit low-energy lightbulbs—when you move, you can always take them with you (although that could be considered a bit stingy). An energy-saving bulb can use one-sixth of the electricity and last twelve times as long as a conventional bulb. The yearly savings far outweigh the extra cost of the bulb.

● Fit an infrared sensor switch to turn on and off the lights, such as exterior security lights (these devices do not work with low-energy bulbs), that are used infrequently. No more fumbling for light switches in the dark.

● Buy a portable electricity monitor. This gadget has two parts. The first part connects to your electricity meter and sends a signal to the second part, which can be carried around the home. The latter tells you how much electricity is being used at any one moment, alerting you to lights, stereo equipment, and any other appliances left on. It can save you up to 25% of your electricity bill.

● Buy appliances that bear the Energy Star logo. These products, which include everything from battery chargers to refrigerators and hot water heaters, have been certified by the Department of Energy and the Environmental Protection Agency as highly energy efficient. The purchase price can be relatively high in some cases, but the savings in utility bills are considerable—up to 30%.

HEATING/COOLING

● Get your furnace/air conditioning system serviced at least once a year; it will run more efficiently.

● Encase your hot water tank in an insulating blanket; this can save around 75% of the average heat lost. If the outside of the tank feels warm, you must insulate it. Remember to insulate the hot water pipes, too.

● Seal up drafts. Amazingly, drafts account for 15% of the heat loss from a typical home. Fit foam or metal weather strips to the edges of windows and exterior doors; a door sweep can be fixed to the bottom of an exterior door on the inside. Apply caulking to cracks around window frames or anywhere else there is a draft.

● If your heating system uses radiators, fit each one with a thermostatic radiator valve, which will respond to the temperature in that room, giving you more control over the heating than if one thermostat governs the whole system.

● Install ceiling fans as alternatives to air conditioning. Clever use of fans in tandem with cross ventilation can reduce the need for artificial cooling. And by reversing the fan in winter (clockwise instead of counterclockwise), you can pull trapped warm air down from the ceiling; this is especially effective in rooms with high ceilings.

WATER

● Check your toilet to see if the cistern leaks. Put a few drops of food coloring in the cistern; if the color seeps into the bowl, you have a leak. Getting it fixed could save up to 250 gallons of water a month.

● If your toilet is old, replace it with a modern low-flush or dual-flush model. Low-flush toilets use only about 11/2 gallons of water per flush, as compared with 3 or more gallons in older toilets; and dual-flush types offer an extra-low option of 1 gallon or less.

LIFESTYLE CHANGES
HIGH COST

THESE TIPS ARE FOR THE SERIOUSLY COMMITTED AND THOSE AIMING TOWARD A TOTAL ECO-REFURBISHMENT. I HAVE KEPT THEM SHORT, FOR THE TECHNOLOGY IN MANY OF THESE AREAS IS DEVELOPING FAST; AND SO EACH PURCHASING DECISION SHOULD BE THOROUGHLY RESEARCHED BEFORE PROCEEDING—THE INTERNET OR A TRADE SHOW IS A GOOD PLACE TO START.

ELECTRICITY

● Fit external or internal, plantation shutters to your windows; they will reduce any heat gain from the sun to keep rooms cooler during summer and cut back any heat loss in winter.

● Cut down on the need for tumble drying by building a covered area or lean-to for airing washing naturally.

● Install a new lighting system throughout your home, using a mixture of low-energy bulbs, light-emitting diodes (LEDs), and compact fluorescent tubes.

● Look into generating your own electricity. Fit either photovoltaic panels or a wind turbine—but only if you live somewhere very exposed and windy—to your roof. (See the section on renewable energies, pages 41–43.)

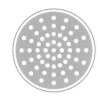

HEATING/COOLING

● If your furnace is over 15 years old, it is probably inefficient. Fit a modern condensing furnace, which may be over 90% efficient.

● Insulate your attic (see page 81 for organic sheep's wool, the best eco insulating product).

● Insulate your walls with external, internal, or cavity wall insulation. It is imperative you tackle this, as 35% of all heat loss occurs through walls.

● Insulate your floors. This can be done to suspended floors and to solid concrete floors, which draw heat away from a room.

● Fit infloor heating using an energy-saving water-heating system. It creates a comfortable environment in which heat rises evenly. By eliminating the need for registers or unsightly radiators, it facilitates furnishing your home; and it reduces the need for wall-to-wall carpeting, with its attendant dust buildup.

● Have your existing windows replaced with double-glazed (or double-pane) windows—the more efficient alternative to storm windows. Those made with low-E (for emissivity) glass are the most effective, as they reflect heat back to its source (your heating system in winter, the sun in summer), but without reducing the light. In some of these windows, the space between the two panes is filled with argon gas, for extra insulation. Choose windows with wood frames, which is less damaging than aluminum or vinyl and will last as long if properly maintained.

WATER

● Move your water heater closer to the area where you use the most hot water. This means you do not have to leave the faucet on for such a long time before the water flows hot.

● Fit low flow faucets to your kitchen and bathroom sinks. These faucets aerate the flow of water to give the effect of a greater flow rate, but use less water.

● Replace your showerhead with a low-flow model, which will send out droplets of water that drench you luxuriously but which saves up to 40% on conventional shower water usage.

● Replace your conventional water heater with a tankless water heating system. This can reduce your energy costs for heating water by up to 50%.

● Use a gray water system that will reuse bath and shower water for flushing toilets.

RENEWABLE ENERGIES

Harnessing the nonpolluting energy that occurs naturally around us makes a whole lot of sense. Why pay good money to excavate and burn finite fossil fuels when we can gather power from renewable sources such as the sun, wind, and water for free? However, in reality it is not that cheap, for the start-up costs for harnessing these forms of energy can be high. Furthermore, we are encouraged to buy our resources from the conventional power suppliers through the convenient pipes and cables they feed into our homes. For people living in towns and cities, it is often not feasible to hook a wind turbine to a roof or balcony.

There is a general misconception that in order to have a truly eco-conscious home you must have a gleaming, shiny (and fast-spinning) wind turbine proudly strapped to your roof. If the truth be known, many of the technologies used to capture these renewable energy sources are yet to be as efficient as their manufacturers (and retailers) claim, and with high purchase and installation costs, the payback periods are long.

In time this will change, but for now it is worth doing your research and speaking to those who have already installed any renewable energy device that may have pricked your eco-conscience. On the plus side, many environmentally friendly home improvements qualify for federal or state tax rebates, which can significantly reduce their cost. In some cases, such as installing a low-flow toilet, this may cover the whole amount. Check with the relevant government agency.

The general feeling among experts is that the wisest investment is in making your home as efficient as possible. Super-insulate all walls, roofs, floors, and openings. Make your home airtight by sealing up any drafts around doors, windows, and chimneys, while ensuring some degree of natural ventilation in each room. Fit storm window to insulate all windows and install the most efficient appliances you can afford. Only once you have made your home efficient should you start to think about investing money in renewable energies; otherwise you are simply pouring your money through a leaky sieve. However, it is helpful to know the basics of each system so you can make informed choices.

Of the methods suggested, solar water heating is considered the most viable, giving you up to 50% of your hot water and having the shortest payback period. Next photovoltaics offer a good solution to reducing your electrical needs, and technology is set to make this increasingly efficient. Biomass furnaces are likely to become smaller and more domestically friendly in years to come, so it is worth considering them as an option for low CO_2 energy. Other solutions, such as wind turbines and ground source heat pumps, are perhaps best used in a remote area where you may not be connected to the electrical grid and need to produce your own energy or must pay a high price to have it installed—so making the payback period more reasonable.

OPPOSITE Making the most of natural light by keeping windows clean and bouncing light off internal surfaces can help keep your fuel and electricity usage down.

PASSIVE SOLAR GAINS

The good news is that, in some small way, your home already soaks up energy from the sun via the materials it is made of; this is known as "passive solar gains." What you need to learn is how to manage and maximize its benefits.

Any of the sun's rays that hit the outside or inside of your home create heat. In the summer this can make your home too hot, but, if maximized, in the winter it can help to reduce the amount of energy needed to heat your home. The two most common ways to soak up the heat from the sun are through windows and sunrooms. However, the problem is that they are also the means by which a home loses the most heat or becomes overheated. If you follow these basic principles, you can get your home to work a little harder for you and can keep it more comfortable all year round.

TO PREVENT HEAT LOSS AND CAPTURE HEAT FROM THE SUN

● On the south side of your home use dense flooring materials, such as stone or ceramic tiles, which have a higher thermal mass, to soak up and store any heat that comes through your glazing. It is released slowly throughout the day. Pile carpets and wooden floorboards have a lower thermal mass, because they are not so dense and so they do not store heat.

● If possible, reduce the windows on the north side of your home to a minimum, and make sure they are double glazed, while still letting in some light, since no direct sunlight will enter your home on this side.

● Cover windows at night with thick draperies, blinds, or shutters.

● If you have a sunroom, you should have a door between it and the rest of the house, which will help you control heat coming in or going out in the winter.

● Fit additional glazing to your windows; this may be temporary, proprietary, or double glazing (of which low e-argon filled units are most efficient).

TO PREVENT OVERHEATING

● Plant a deciduous tree outside your south-facing windows. When its leaves are out in the summer, it will naturally shade your home from the sun; and in the winter it will allow the lower winter sun to shine through its bare branches allowing heat in. Isn't nature clever.

● Fit external or internal, plantation, shutters on your windows. By opening the windows and closing the shutters, you can minimize heat from the sun, and the adjustable slats of plantation shutters allow you to control the daylight also.

● Fit venetian blinds, which allow you to control the amount of sunlight entering the room, reducing the intense summer sun and allowing in the weaker winter sun.

● If you're planning to add a sunroom to your house, resist the temptation to choose one with a glass roof. A solid roof (which can also be insulated) will deflect the high summer sun, while the glass walls will admit the low winter sun, effectively warming the space.

● Ventilate your home properly; this can be as simple as opening windows on both sides of your home to allow airflow or even using an extractor fan (but the latter will use energy and cost you money).

SOLAR WATER HEATING

A solar water heating unit—using energy from the sun—works alongside your conventional heating system to provide hot water for use in bathrooms and kitchens and even (if your central heating system uses hot water, rather than air) to heat your home. Over a year, solar water heating can, depending on your climate, provide 50% or more of your hot water needs.

There are various kinds of solar water heating systems, but they can be divided into two basic types: active and passive. Both types include a solar collector and one or more storage tanks.

THE SOLAR COLLECTOR—which is usually placed on the roof and faces south. For domestic applications this typically takes the form of a large, rectangular, glass-fronted panel. Another kind consists of a series of long glass tubes (called evacuated tubes, because the air has been withdrawn from them). Yet another form, called an integrated collector-storage, or batch, system, consists of a glazed box containing the storage tank.

In an active system, a pump circulates the water through the collector—or in some cases, circulates a heat-transfer fluid, such as antifreeze, which, by means of a heat exchanger, heats the water. A passive system has no moving parts but exploits the fact that hot water rises, pushing cold water down).

THE WATER STORAGE TANK—which may be located within the house or, in the case of passive systems, on the roof. This must be well insulated.

You will also need a conventional "backup" water heating system for times, such as rainy, wintry days, when the solar heat is not adequate. Some solar heating systems include this additional supply component. Even with its limitations, however, solar water heating is generally considered to be the most efficient way to incorporate renewable energy into your home.

GEOTHERMAL HEAT PUMPS

These pumps use the natural resource of heat in the ground to heat your home—and also, if desired, to cool it in the summer and to heat your water supply. Whereas the air temperature may reach extremes of below 0°F in the winter and 100°F or more in the summer, the ground temperature just a few feet below the surface will remain fairly constant all year round.

There are several different types of geothermal heating system. All of them use a loop of plastic pipe, which is buried in the ground or in water (which, like the earth, maintains a relatively constant temperature), and a heat pump, which transfers heat from the loop to the building—or vice versa for air conditioning.

CLOSED LOOP SYSTEMS—are so called because the fluid circulating within the pipe, an environmentally friendly antifreeze, does not come into contact with the surrounding earth (or water). In horizontal closed loop systems, the trench required for the piping is relatively shallow—about 4–8 ft.—but must accommodate between 400 and 600 linear feet of pipe. The area required can be reduced by using the "slinky" arrangement, in which the pipe is laid in overlapping coils. If there is a nearby pond of sufficient depth, the pipe can be submerged in this. Where ground space is extremely limited, a vertical closed loop system can be used. This entails drilling several deep "wells," ranging from 150 to 450 ft., for the pipes and is naturally more expensive.

OPEN LOOP SYSTEMS—are so called because the liquid circulating in the pipes is drawn from a body of water, such as a stream or pond, and flows into the heat exchanger in the pump and out again.

HEAT EXCHANGERS—are basically of two types: fluid to air and fluid to water. The first kind is used with a forced-air system, whereas the second can be used to provide radiant, or infloor, heating and cooling or a hot-water heating system (which uses radiators). Either type of heat exchanger can be used to supply hot water.

The high cost of installing a geothermal system can be recouped within five to ten years through savings on your utility bill. And because the system is so energy efficient, it will significantly reduce your carbon footprint.

PHOTOVOLTAICS

Solar PV or photovoltaic panels convert simple daylight—energy from the sun—through layers of silicon into electrical energy, which can then be used in the home. Because they do not actually need to be exposed to the sun, they create energy even on a cloudy day.

Positioned on a roof, in order to pick up the most energy the panels will ideally be oriented toward the path of the sun—in the U. S. this is in a southerly direction. The direct current (DC) electricity—similar to that which comes from a battery—produced by the panels can either be sold on to the local utility company via an inverter and an export meter or stored in a battery before being altered through an inverter to an alternating current (AC), which can then be used as mains power within your home (called an off-grid system).

Most photovoltaic panels take the form of surface-mounted modules, although some manufacturers are producing less conspicuous versions, in the form of roof tiles—resembling ordinary terracotta or gray slate tiles. If you choose the former, the panels will have a visual impact on your home, so you will need to check your local building codes before fitting them. In addition they can be very heavy, so it is best to make totally sure that your roof can actually support them. Seek the opinion of an engineer or experienced building contractor.

The great thing about photovoltaic panels is that they produce CO_2-free electricity. However, the main drawbacks are the cost of the panels and their relative effectiveness. In some cases, the payback period may be longer than the estimated 30-year lifespan of the units themselves. This could change if the units become more efficient, the cost of electricity rises substantially, or the panels simply become cheaper to buy. That being said, you may be able to get a tax credit for installing a photovoltaic system.

WIND TURBINES

Wind turbines use a system of propellers to convert energy from the wind into electricity. These can either be positioned on a tall mast away from any buildings or mounted on a roof. In general, they are mounted on a tower above building height in order to catch the faster moving streams of wind. Location is critical to the efficiency of a wind turbine; it must be free from obstructions, such as buildings or trees, and, ideally, located in an area that has a good consistent average wind speed. Before you invest in one, it is worth measuring the average wind speed of your area with an anemometer (wind speed gauge) for as long as possible—preferably over one year—because the more wind that can be harvested, the more electricity will be produced. An average wind speed of at least 20 feet per second is needed to make a wind turbine viable. Local meteorological offices will hold information on local wind speeds, which you can compare against your own data, to help you calculate how much energy your turbine will create and whether it will save you money.

Wind turbines create direct current (DC) power, which must be put through an inverter to create an alternating current (AC); this can then be used directly as mains power or stored in a large battery. Power output varies, depending on the size of the turbine, but a typical domestic model will create between 1 and 6 kilowatts. Like photovoltaic panels, turbines can also be connected to the electrical grid, which means you can actually sell any excess energy back to the electricity companies via a special inverter and meter system. This may sound great in theory; but in practice, things like your fridge and freezer are likely to use up most of the energy produced.

Although the presence of a wind turbine is a pleasure for some peoplpe, others are quite set against them and any noise that they may produce. So you must check your local building codes before installing one.

BIOMASS HEAT SYSTEMS

Biomass furnaces and stoves act in a similar way to conventional heating systems, but instead of being powered by fossil fuels, they draw energy from natural materials, typically maize—hence their alternative name "corn furnace"—or wood, in the form of chips or pellets. Other materials include sugar cane and animal waste (generally for industrial installations).

A variety of different stoves and furnaces are designed to burn biomass fuels: small stand-alone, or in-room, stoves; forced-air furnaces; and add-on furnaces to be used in conjunction with a conventional furnace. Biomass furnaces have a large storage container, or hopper, which gradually feeds in the fuel supply. Although the furnaces naturally occupy a lot of space, the in-room stoves are fairly compact and can serve as an attractive focal point in a living room or kitchen.

Unlike other renewable energy sources, such as wind and sun, biomass fuel must be paid for by the consumer. Moreover, some of the furnaces are quite expensive to buy and/or install. However, biomass fuel will effectively supply you with a very low CO_2-producing heating system, as you will be re-emitting only the CO_2 already soaked up by the material in its production, thereby saving your home from directly producing around 6 tons of CO_2 each year.

MATERIALS

ECO-MATERIALS

TOO MANY PEOPLE HOLD THE FALSE VIEW THAT IMPLEMENTING AN ENVIRONMENTALLY FRIENDLY DESIGN WILL INEVITABLY LEAD TO A COMPROMISE IN STYLE; A LIMITED UNDERSTANDING OF THE AVAILABLE ECO-MATERIALS SERVES ONLY TO COMPOUND THIS MISCONCEPTION.

Traditional eco-materials such as hemp and sheep's wool are considered by many to be coarse, nondurable, and outdated. But beyond the traditional, there is a new generation of advanced materials that not only hold excellent sustainable credentials but also have a wonderful tactile quality and can help our homes to become stylishly eco-chic.

Understanding eco-materials—what the options are, how they are made, how to use them—is key to creating a home that is at once functional, beautiful, and environmentally aware. This chapter opens up the creative possibilities to those who wish to design eco- interiors but will not compromise on style.

All too often, when I see eco-homes I despair at a heavy-handed reliance on a single material, such as wood, which actually diminishes the design and detracts from the quality of the material; sometimes you metaphorically cannot see the wood for the trees. Using a combination of materials—and you do not need that many—can give a home a feeling of space and lightness, as well as providing an opportunity to create focus or drama.

ABOVE Using an eco-wallpaper can help you to reduce your home's toxin levels by cutting out petrochemical-laden paints and inks.

Although I am not usually one to generalize, there is a common aspect to each category of eco-materials, from the factory-made and technologically advanced, through the natural and sustainable, to the vintage and recycled. By understanding the nature of each category, you can appreciate the way an urban eco-chic interior can be brought together—layering surface finishes to create a complete look without an overreliance on any single material.

An interior that relies solely on technological materials can lack character; furnished only with sleek surfaces, a space can be devoid of real focus. Just think back to those gleaming white kitchens of science fiction films to be reminded of how soulless an interior can be. However, technologically advanced materials can provide a backdrop for natural and recycled materials to come to the fore and be truly appreciated; they can act as the canvas on which the artwork is grounded.

Likewise, if an interior employs too much of one specific natural material—for example, wood—it can be equally overwhelming. This may be fine in a log cabin, but for a more sophisticated interior, the ideal is a contrast of textures, with technological and vintage materials highlighting the warmth and irregular qualities that a natural product such as wood has to offer.

When an interior is filled with vintage materials and recycled pieces, it is often full of quirky character, but it may languish in nostalgia. A heavy reliance on vintage can point to a lack of ambition to create a truly contemporary space. The layers of age and the piecemeal quality of recycled materials can feel tired and stuffy—as if a fear of the here and now has taken hold.

Balance underpins urban eco-chic, combining technology to create clean, efficient spaces; nature to give a grounding warmth and texture; and vintage elements to impart identity and soul. In this way, you can create livable interiors that are as functional as they are good-looking, as healthy as they are environmentally conscious. Now that is what I call urban eco-chic.

The following sections within this chapter present a choice of the most stylish eco-materials currently available. Alongside each description, I have stated which category of the urban eco-chic principle the material sits within—indicating the stylistic effect it will have. This will help you to achieve the desired balance between technology, nature, and vintage.

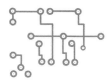

MATERIAL **PARTS**

IN ACCORDANCE WITH THE
URBAN ECO-CHIC TRIUMVIRATE,
ECO-MATERIALS FIT BROADLY
INTO THE TECHNOLOGY, NATURE,
OR VINTAGE CATEGORIES.
EACH HAS ITS OWN UNIQUE
CHARACTERISTICS, WHICH ARE
DESCRIBED HERE, AND CAN BE
USED IN VARYING RATIOS,
DEPENDING ON THE ROOM BEING
DECORATED, TO CREATE THE
PERFECT ECO-CHIC INTERIOR.

TECHNOLOGICALLY ADVANCED ECO-MATERIALS

Such materials are often factory made, with a high quality of finish, offering a clean, crisp, and contemporary style. They may well look like many other conventional products, but these eco-materials will have been made using low-energy techniques or technologically advanced methods that use natural or recycled materials in their content.

Technologically developed materials add a level of precision to your home and in many cases can help to reduce your energy or resources usage during their lifespan. This can counteract the relatively high level of embodied energy (see page 51) created in their manufacture, transportation, and fitting.

Materials such as linoleum, bio-polymer resins, and layered insulating sheet are all examples of technologically advanced materials. You can specify any of these products confident that its performance, reliability, and environmental footprint have been carefully considered.

NATURAL OR SUSTAINABLE ECO-MATERIALS

When well managed, naturally occurring eco-materials are easily replenished, thereby minimizing their environmental impact. Materials such as wood, wool, cork, and bamboo are excellent examples of natural materials that can be produced in a sustainable manner and benefit the home.

Prone to surface variations in both color and texture, natural materials have a unique or customized quality, adding a material richness to an interior. Generally they have a grain or fiber, which is an inherent part of their character. From a design perspective, natural materials lend a grounding quality to a space, offering a relaxing warmth, which helps us to reconnect to ourselves and nature as a whole. Unlike many artificial products, natural materials such as wood and leather age well, gaining character with use.

When left untreated by chemical finishes, natural materials are free from toxins that can off-gas. Some may even have natural antibacterial qualities. As a further benefit, they will be breathable, allowing moisture to pass through, and so help to manage condensation and the prevention of damp within the home.

VINTAGE AND RECYCLED ECO-MATERIALS

Using vintage items within an interior scheme is, in my opinion, a valid form of recycling, for you are saving perfectly serviceable materials or furniture from entering landfill. But there are, of course, more conventional recycled materials, which are created anew from discarded items.

Recycled materials frequently wear their eco-credentials on their sleeves, so can be easily identified. Made from reprocessed products, they often take on a mottled appearance. As recycling processes improve, the quality and design of such materials are becoming more refined. Instead of being made up of a dozen or more contrasting-colored parts, they can consist of fewer tonal shades, offering a different and, for some, more visually pleasing look.

Products labeled as recycled may be made up of a relatively low percentage of reprocessed materials. Manufacturers may apply the term when a product has a recycled content of 40% or more, with up to 60% being made up of new materials. For me, this figure is too low.

Materials that are easily recyclable, such as polypropylene, also fall within this category. Ease of recyclability may indicate a high recycled content, but not always. Materials with a high recycled content and easy recyclability include glass-stone, stainless steel, and some plastics.

ABOVE When I came to decorate my own living room, the eco-credentials of each material were foremost in my mind—from the eco-friendly paints applied to the walls to the recycled glass stone used to create the kitchen surfaces and the round tabletop.

ECO-CRITERIA

No matter which category—technology, nature, or vintage—an eco material falls into, when discussing it, there are key terms to be aware of;

EMBODIED ENERGY is the energy taken to extract, produce, transport, and fit a material to the point of its intended use. Measured in kilowatt hours per yard cubed (kWh/yd.^{3}), these calculations enable us to compare the relative environmental merits of materials and products. If steel is shipped a vast distance from its place of manufacture, it will have a high embodied energy compared with locally sourced lumber, which will have a low embodied energy. Although difficult to calculate accurately, a comparative index of the environmental impact of materials is a priority.

LIFE-CYCLE ANALYSIS takes into account not only the embodied energy of a material but its whole life cost, from production, through usage and, finally, disposal. This analysis helps us understand how great an impact each material has on the environment, taking into account its durability and recyclability.

CRADLE-TO-CRADLE materials are those considered from an environmental perspective throughout their life cycle—in other words, a material that is produced in a well-managed, sustainable manner from a renewable source, used efficiently, and then recycled easily at the end of its useful life, ready to become a raw material for another use. By contrast, if the life cycle of a material is not considered, it will finally, and wastefully, be put into landfill; so this is known as a cradle-to-grave material.

ECO-**FLOORS**

WHEN CHOOSING YOUR IDEAL
FLOORING, YOU WILL BE
BALANCING FUNCTION AND
STYLE WITH COST, AS FLOOR
AREAS MAKE A SUBSTANTIAL
IMPACT ON ANY BUDGET.
ALSO, IT WILL NOT SURPRISE
YOU TO LEARN THAT FLOORS
AFFECT THE ENVIRONMENTAL
IMPACT OF YOUR HOME—
BOTH INSIDE AND OUT.

Within the home, flooring surfaces can absorb warmth from the sun—good in winter, bad in summer—or insulate against heat loss. Their color and surface texture can bounce light around a space, cutting back on the need for artificial light. The correct flooring materials may also improve air quality, enhancing a "healthy" home, whereas the wrong surfaces may trap dust, aggrevate allergies, and release toxins over time.

Similarly, your choice of floor materials affects the environment outside your home. For instance, choosing a hardwood floor may contribute to the destruction of delicate ecosystems or fund illegal logging practices. The production of plastics may create unnecessary levels of pollution, while their transportation from far-flung locations contributes to a higher carbon footprint.

Lastly, their disposal (and cheaper flooring may not last as long) may release trapped toxins into the environment during the degrading process at landfill. Encouragingly, there are a surprising number of beautiful, environmentally conscious flooring options for every style, budget, and spatial concept—so you need not feel limited.

OPPOSITE A selection of eco-flooring solutions (clockwise from top left): natural pebble tiles, bamboo, FSC-certified wood, cork tiles, sisal, and recycled rubber.

LINOLEUM

Linoleum is made from natural, renewable materials including linseed oil, wood or cork flour, and flax, laid onto a natural, fiber backing such as canvas or burlap.

It has no artificial chemicals, so is good for keeping toxin levels low. Being a hard-wearing, smooth surface, it is easy to clean without trapping dust. It also has a natural antibacterial agent: it off-gases linseed oil, which exterminates germs but is nontoxic to humans.

Linoleum is available in a range of colors, in both a continuous roll, to create seamless surfaces, and as individual tiles, which can be laid in a variety of patterns. It is an ideal material for kitchens, bathrooms, hallways, and any other spaces that come into regular contact with water.

NATURAL RUBBER

Natural rubber flooring is made from the latex sap of rubber trees, which is extracted by scoring the bark and allowing the sap to seep out. Once collected, the yellow latex is mixed with other natural materials and pigments, then heated, pressure treated, and finally cut into tiles. Scraps from factories are conveniently recycled: they are shredded and mixed to create flooring for sports facilities and also acoustic and thermal insulation.

Only 10% of rubber flooring on the market is natural. Manufacturers claim it is a carbon-positive material because rubber trees take so much carbon from the atmosphere as they grow that this outweighs any put back through its manufacture and transportation. Natural rubber gives off no toxic fumes.

Available in a wide variety of colors and surface textures, natural rubber flooring has great design potential. It is often used in primary colors and so can feel hi-tech or even playful and naïve. But if specified with a smooth surface and in a natural, muted shade, it can feel more sophisticated, which makes it perfect for urban kitchens and bathrooms.

Being highly durable, waterproof, and easy to clean inatural rubber can, like lino, be used in wet spaces and areas of high traffic, such as hallways.

Its surface, which makes it nonslip and also absorbs impact and noise. However, rubber can sustain dents if furniture is placed directly on top of it, and scuffs can show up on the smoother types.

RECYCLED RUBBER

Recycled rubber floors are made of both postindustrial and virgin rubber chips.

Like the other rubber products, it is available as tiles or in rolls and must be laid directly onto a smooth floor surface, using adhesive.

Available in a limited range of neutral colors, recycled rubber flooring has (as with many recycled materials) a mottled quality when seen in close proximity. Due to its mixed contents, variations in color do occur, but since the surface is formed of different-colored chips, this is barely noticable.

Tough, durable, and with good nonslip qualities, recycled rubber flooring is ideal for areas of high traffic. However, this material does yellow when exposed to direct sunlight.

RECYCLED RUBBER MATTING

Worn bus tires are difficult to dispose of in an environmentally friendly manner. However, a manufacturer in the United States has developed a process whereby these tires are chopped up and wire-brushed down to expose the nylon fibers they contain. The resulting material is then bonded together (although, sadly, with a polyurethane glue) to create a chenille-like mosaic of recycled rubber matting.

Its extended life makes it a good environmental choice and an alternative to the conventional polypropylene, but it does have a high embodied energy within its production. For customers outside the United States, its carbon footprint is increased because of the transportation involved.

Available as carpet tile squares or in rolls, the matting comes in a variety of colors, all with a black rubber background. This flooring is incredibly durable and surprisingly soft, which makes it useful in high-traffic areas. Being made of rubber, it can be used both inside and out.

CARPET TILES

Various construction methods are used to produce carpet tiles; but typically fibers are tufted onto a natural, fiber backing material, such as hemp, cotton, or linen, which is then coated with latex to hold the fibers in place. A bitumen backing is applied to give the tile strength and rigidity.

Although they have a relatively high embodied energy, due to their production, carpet tiles are long lasting and can be reconditioned and reused. If discarded, they can be burned to produce energy.

Carpet tiles are extremely hard-wearing and can be replaced when worn or damaged. They are easy to install and can be laid straight onto a floor using double-sided tape or a special adhesive, cutting the expense of fitting. Since they can be laid individually, carpet tiles are a flexible option in difficult-to-access areas. A familiar sight in offices, their ever more sophisticated range of colours and styles now makes them a real option for home.

PAPER RUGS

Paper rugs are stronger and more hard-wearing than you might imagine. Fabricated solely from sustainable materials, they are made from the soft wood pulp of coniferous trees. The paper is mixed with a resin and then made into a yarn, which is woven onto a natural jute or latex backing.

They are available in a selection of natural soft browns to grays with a greater variety of broader trim colors. Despite being flexible and durable, they are best used in areas of light to medium wear, but not on stairways or under furniture on casters

ABOVE These simple wooden floorboards add a rustic charm to this bedroom, providing a textural backdrop for the clean lines of the bed and other furniture.

CORK

Cut by hand from the bark of the cork oak tree, cork actually grows back over 8–10 years when it is ready for further harvesting. It truly is a sensational sustainable material, and a firm favorite of designers from the early modernists of the 1920s to the present day.

Cork has a closed-cell honeycomb-like structure, which makes it warm to the touch, water resistant, and a good thermal insulator and gives it natural bounce. Besides being easy to clean, cork is durable, with a natural insect resistance called suberin and an antiallergenic quality. All these properties make it a great choice for domestic flooring.

Cork flooring is available as square tiles and also laminated to a wooden subbase to create tongue-and-groove panels. Dyed either dark or lighter natural shades, cork can create a luxurious effect, with the added benefit that the paler shades help to reflect light back into a space.

Conventionally used in bathrooms and kitchens, cork is now chic enough to be used in bedrooms and living rooms as well.

BAMBOO

Bamboo is a grass; so when it is harvested, its roots simply regrow another shoot, dispensing with the need to replant seeds and preventing soil erosion. It grows at exceptional speed—as opposed to 15–25 years for timber, bamboo is ready to cut in 3–5 years—without the need for pesticides.

Planks are made from the solid outer edge of the bamboo stalk, which is cut into very precise thin strips and laminated together to form solid boards. The tight grain structure creates a tough surface, and the laminated strips can lie horizontally or vertically. When they are laid horizontally the regular rhythm of the bamboo knots is shown, whereas laid vertically they produce a smooth knot-free floor. For higher traffic areas, bamboo can be turned into a thin thread, which is bonded together with a resin to create a floor that is twice as tough and resistant to the impact of even stiletto heels.

Bamboo is available only in a limited color range and generally comes with a pre-finished lacquer, so you cannot stain it yourself. Due to its speed of growth and availability, bamboo is more affordable than hardwood, which makes it one of the cheapest natural floorings available. The only drawback is that production is largely in the Far East, so it has a higher embodied energy through transporation than a locally sourced wood floor.

WOOD

All wood products should be sourced from a sustainable, well-managed supply. One of the most widely recognized groups that certify sustainable management is the Forest Stewardship Council (FSC). Buying FSC-certified wood and products supports the environmentally responsible, socially beneficial, and economically viable management of the world's forests. It ensures the protection not only of the forest itself but also of the huge biodiversity affected by logging. If not carefully managed, logging can have a disastrous effect on a forest and, on a greater scale, global climate change. This book is printed on paper from FSC-certified lumber, so see page 4 for the FSC logo.

By replacing high embodied energy materials such as steel, the use of wood can reduce the carbon footprint of homes and the number of toxins present within them. Moreover, wood is a biodegradable material that, when used thoughtfully, can be recycled or will decompose naturally.

SOLID WOOD

A material familiar to us all, solid wood flooring brings a natural warmth to any home. Its textural quality is grounding and calming. To reduce the carbon footprint of the wood, it should ideally be from as local a source as possible and not from the other side of the globe.

Wood floors are available as soft- or hardwood planks, tongue-and-groove boards, and parquet tiles. Many beautiful wood floors are supplied pre-finished with a lacquer or polyurethane coating, which can contain off-gassing VOCs, so check before you buy. The natural beauty of wood is best brought out through the use of natural waxes and oils, such as Danish oil, which give it a soft luster with no off-gassing toxins. Buy the flooring unfinished and treat it yourself. Although it is very hard-wearing, solid wood is prone to scratches and dents; but as with any solid material, the marks can be sanded out.

Finally, as a natural material, wood is prone to expansion and shrinkage, depending on moisture conditions. Leave wood in your home for up to two weeks prior to fitting to ensure it is acclimatized.

ENGINEERED WOOD

Made from layers of a combination of soft- and hardwoods, engineered wood floors have advantages and disadvantages over those made from solid wood. On the plus side, they can be made up of entirely FSC-certified wood using only a small quantity of slower-growing hardwood and a core layer of less expensive softwood, taken from faster-growing forests. Also, the core layer can be made from smaller pieces than the surface layer, so it is a more efficient use of the wood and reduces waste.

As a composite, engineered wood has flexibility in terms of available sizes and is less prone to the effects of humidity and warping than solid wood. If dented, engineered wood can be sanded down and refinished, though the result depends on the depth of the dent and that of the top hardwood layer.

On the downside, engineered wood does not have as long a life span as solid wood. Also it has a higher embodied energy due to the manufacturing process. Because of its greater number of component parts, it is also harder to recycle and cannot be reused so readily. Lastly, the bonding agent is likely to be a formaldehyde resin glue, which will, over time, off-gas toxins into your home. So if it were my home, I would opt for the solid wood flooring and swallow the extra cost.

STONE TILES

Provided they are cut from a local source, stone tiles are a viable environmental material. As a naturally occurring substance, stone is mined from the earth, cut, and then polished; no carbon-heavy firing process is necessary, as it is with ceramic tiles. Stone can be recycled at the end of its useful life; crushed into smaller pieces, it can be reused within the building industry. Even when deposited in landfill, stone remains inert—it does not produce toxins or release methane. Shipping stone tiles vast distances massively increases its embodied energy, so look online to see what types of stone are mined near you and work this into your interior scheme.

Stone tiles have a natural, variegated color and surface texture; the material's strength gives durability and longevity wherever it is used. If you have only a small floor area to tile, search reclamation yards and salvage sites for materials that may be left over from other building projects that you can buy cheaply.

With stone it is best to specify a honed finish, which gives it a softer, matte look, to bring out the natural quality of the surface. A highly polished gloss finish can make stone look as though it has been coated with a shiny polyurethane layer.

PEBBLE TILES

Simple, soft rounded pebbles are collected by hand from beaches in India and Indonesia, their bases ground flat, and fixed with adhesive to a backing sheet to form tiles. Once laid and grouted, the tiles' smooth surface and natural color variations work to create a calm feel within a space.

Although these pebble tiles have a low-level manufacturing energy attached to them, they are transported vast distances from their point of manufacture, which increases their embodied energy. Furthermore, picking pebbles from beaches is not encouraged in many regions, as it can in effect cause coastal erosion.

Once laid with a grout, these tiles cannot be taken up and reused. However, but as a natural material that requires no surface finish or coloration, if put in landfill they are relatively inert and so will not break down to create any polluting toxins.

Being highly textured yet so hard wearing, these natural pebble tiles work brilliantly in areas of high traffic, such as hallways. But they are also a good choice where a bit of sensory impact is desirable—for example, in a bathroom.

RIGHT This vintage rug ties in with the well-traveled suitcases and wool throws and also provides a warm surface to step onto when you get in and out of bed. Due to its age, it is unlikely to have been treated with the cocktail of toxins that modern rugs often contain.

RUGS

In order to reduce the effects of dust and mites, combine hard flooring with a softer surface, such as a natural or vintage rug, which can be used to zone an area within a room. Most of the natural floor coverings mentioned in this section, such as sisal and coir, can be made into an edged rug. Rather than pay a lot of money for a custom-made floor rug, buy a piece of natural flooring to fit the dimensions of your space, and have it finished with a fabric or leather trim.

Another option is ethnic rugs. If you are happy to live with their colorful style, it is worth remembering that hand-made ethnic rugs crafted in remote areas may well not have been treated with the normal cocktail of commercial fire retardants and chemicals. An alternative is to buy vintage or antique rugs from markets or antique shops, which may have been made before the introduction of fire retardants. Their age and wear add character to your home and a sense of luxury or nostalgia.

NATURAL WOOL CARPET

Pure wool fibers—the history of which should be checked for any possible chemical contamination—are woven onto a natural, fiber backing, such as linen or cotton, which in turn is backed with a natural latex rubber. But be sure to specify 100% *natural* wool carpet and not simply 100% wool carpet as the latter may contain toxins in its artificial latex backing.

Unlike artificial fibers, sheep's wool fleece contains lanolin, which acts as a natural stain inhibitor; and due to its ability to absorb moisture,

LEFT Herringbone wood strips create a hard-wearing yet warm entrance-hall floor. The wood can easily be recycled, extending its useful life.

BELOW Coir natural flooring is a sophisticated choice of covering. Although coir and sisal are not as soft underfoot as wool, they are warmer to the touch than a solid wood or stone floor surface and help to reduce any noise transmission to the space below.

the fleece is also naturally antistatic. At the end of its useful life, pure wool carpet will biodegrade without harm to the environment.

Pure natural wool carpet is perhaps the most hard-wearing and easy to maintain of all the natural soft flooring materials. On the whole, pure natural wool carpets are available in a limited range of pile textures and in a selection of natural shades. Soft and warm underfoot, it is perfect for hallways, bedrooms, and living rooms. As an alternative, pure wool can be blended with flax or sisal to create floor coverings with a fine weave, texture, and strength. A wool-flax blend is softer underfoot, while a wool-sisal blend creates a tweed effect.

With all natural floor coverings, manufacturers recommend using a stain-protection solution at the point of fitting. Natural materials do not react well to water and can mark, so it is important to be aware of the cleaning instructions the moment the carpet is fitted—do not wait for a spillage! Most manufacturers will sell you a care kit, which may prove to be good value; it will certainly be cheaper than replacing a marked carpet.

SISAL

Grown in Africa and South America, sisal is extracted from the agave cactus plant and has traditionally been used in rope making. Sisal is likely to be toxin free, and it uses no artificial backing materials, which might contaminate it. Similar to wool, it is antistatic and will biodegrade at the end of its life.

It is hard-wearing, but coarser to the touch than wool, and so a good choice for hallways and stairs. It is available in a wide range of weaves—from herringbone to bouclé—and in natural colors.

COIR

Often blended with sisal, coir is made in India from the fibers of coconut husks. These are removed by hand, washed, and softened, and then woven into a flooring, after which a latex backing is applied.

Coir is coarse in texture and rough to the touch, but it is hard-wearing and appropriate for use in living rooms and hallways. The threads are chunky and can appear hairy, so it is not a clean, contemporary look. It is available in just a small range of colors and weaves.

JUTE

The stalk of the corchorus plant, in southern India, provides the basis of jute. It has a fine woven texture with a soft sheen. As the least hard-wearing of the natural fiber floor coverings, it is better suited to low traffic areas such as living rooms and bedrooms. It is available in just a small selection of shades and weaves.

SEAGRASS AND MOUNTAIN GRASS

Both seagrass and mountain grass are available as natural-fiber floorings. Although they are affordable, they are not widely used. Often they have wide weaves with a shiny surface texture, which makes them slippery and so inappropriate for use in areas such as stairways, but usable in living rooms, dining rooms, and bedrooms. They are available in a narrow selection of weaves and natural colors, in shades of light brown.

RECLAIMED WOOD PLANKS AND PARQUET

A vast amount of the wood we consume each year heads straight to landfill, where it produces methane—a gas three times more harmful to the environment than CO_2. So finding alternative uses for wood salvaged from old buildings and the construction industry makes far more sense, especially when it is so highly reusable. Diverting wood from landfill reduces the need for new wood to be felled and transported, and with it unnecessary carbon emissions.

Because wood ages well, you are buying a material with an identity that adds depth to interior spaces. Use it on floors, walls, work surfaces—in fact anywhere you might use conventional wood. You have the option of using it either in its original state with an aged surface finish—knocks, dents, and all—or sanding it back to reveal a fresh surface finish.

Unless you have a guaranteed supply from an old building under demolition, using reclaimed wood flooring is something of a lottery; it is a question of what is available at the time you need it. Due to its age and reuse, there is a possibility of woodworm and other damage, so inspect it carefully and treat as appropriate. Search for reclaimed wood and parquet blocks online or, even better, at a local wood recycling center.

ECO-WALLS

TREATING YOUR WALLS IS THE EASIEST AND MOST COST-EFFECTIVE WAY TO IMPACT ON THE LOOK AND FEEL OF A SPACE. BUT EVEN A SEEMINGLY SIMPLE PAINT JOB HAS ENVIRONMENTAL CONSEQUENCES BOTH WITHIN YOUR HOME AND ON THE WIDER WORLD OUTSIDE IT.

Using environmentally friendly wall finishes need not limit what you can do within an interior space, for there is now an excellent variety of eco materials to work with. Even better, nontoxic and sustainable products bring a number of positive benefits that will enhance your home's urban eco-chic feel.

Light-reflective surfaces, such as some recycled plastics, and translucent materials, like glass, can bounce natural light around your home and so reduce the need for additional artificial lighting. Eco-wall coverings, including wood and natural-fiber wallpapers, add impact, character, and texture, while using eco-paints keeps your home smelling sweet and toxin free to create a healthier living space.

Making sure that the materials you use come from a truly sustainable source will mean that when you have finished with them they can either be recycled or will easily biodegrade. By choosing eco-wall treatments, you are enhancing the attractiveness of your home, without sacrificing your personal style, and at the same time showing your commitment to caring for the environment.

OPPOSITE There are a number of exciting eco-friendly wall treatments to choose from (clockwise from top left): an ingenious internal wall made from recycled glass bottles, recycled plastic panels, eco-wallpaper printed with non-toxic inks, oiled lumber paneling, recycled glass tiles, and Ecoresin panels with embedded natural reeds.

ABOVE Contemporary design does not need to be all sharp edges and hard geometry; the uneven wall surface in this living room adds a softness that mimics that of the unstructured sofa.

● ECO- OR NATURAL PAINT

Made from a variety of materials, including water, chalk, natural oils, and clays, natural paints coat walls in breathable, nontoxic color.

Conventional paints are made using petrochemical products. The toxic solvents often used to improve paint flow are known collectively as Volatile Organic Compounds (VOCs). These solvents evaporate off as paint dries and for some time after. Where there is insufficient ventilation VOCs can cause headaches, dizziness and nausea, breathing difficulties, and allergic reactions.

Besides being VOC-free, eco-paints allow moisture to move through walls, preventing damp and saving paint surfaces from cracking. Natural coatings are available as flat finish, eggshell, and clay paints, as well as a range of varnishes, lacquers, and oils. With their quality now comparable to conventional paints there seems little reason—apart from their slightly higher cost—not to use eco- or natural paints.

● INSULATING PAINT

Although certain skeptics within the paint industry question their effectiveness, insulating paints are beginning to come onto the market. By using tiny, hollow glass microspheres (no bigger than a grain of sand), which trap air, they act like a thermos flask to insulate your walls. These microspheres are mixed with normal paint finishes and, without hindering breathability, can be used indoors to trap heat or outdoors to reflect heat. Free of both solvents and VOCs, they may, claim manufacturers, save you up to 25% on your heating bill.

● LIME PLASTER

A traditional building material, long used in Europe, lime plaster is becoming popular with some eco-minded American building contractors—mainly because it is porous, allowing moisture to seep in and evaporate out.

Lime plaster can be used on interior walls in conjunction with breathable finishes such as clay paints. Use lime plaster when re-pointing brickwork to prevent the bricks from retaining moisture and losing their protective face. Lime plaster and mortars are soft and allow for movement; self-heal any small cracks; and ultimately can be removed so the bricks may then be reused.

GLASS

Although glass has a high embodied energy, due to the carbon-heavy manufacturing processes and its weight, glass panels allow natural light to filter through and so reduce the need for artificial lighting. Using glass to create internal partitions within spaces that do not require good acoustic privacy—kitchens, dining rooms, living rooms—makes sense, allowing light to be drawn through the house.

Because the angle of the sun's light changes, glass allows you to create dynamic lighting effects. Use glass screens, blocks, or partitions anywhere light falls onto walls or the floor.

RECYCLED-GLASS TILES

During the manufacturing process, recycled glass is cleaned, crushed, and heated until it reaches crystallization point. At this stage the glass fuses together before being left to cool. Tiles made from colored glass retain the original color—for example, green wine bottles produce green tiles. Tiles made from uncolored glass are often back-painted in a range of colors.

Because they use recycled materials, which would otherwise go to landfill, these tiles are a reasonably eco-friendly option. They have a high embodied energy due to the recycling process, but arguably less than conventional ceramic tiles. Currently, glass tiles are not widely available. Due to the relatively small scale of production, combined with high labor and manufacturing costs, these tiles can be expensive.

Recycled-glass tiles add a contemporary sparkle and translucent quality to kitchens and bathrooms.

OPPOSITE A home office space that uses predominately natural materials. Such materials could overpower a smaller, more enclosed room; but because this study corner is cleverly positioned in an open-plan, flexible space, the wood paneling simply emphasizes the feature wall, while the display shelving adds visual interest.

Although best used on wall surfaces, they can be used on horizontal work surfaces, but not floors.

RECYCLED PLASTIC

Recycling plastics prevents an incredible array of discarded products from going to landfill. The plastics are sorted, cleaned, and chipped into flakes, then, through a combination of heat and pressure, reformed into solid plastic sheets. These sheets have a mottled quality, as the coloration from the recycled materials does not mix. Although some sheets are colorful, the mixes can be made subtler.

Each type of recycled plastic has different properties. For example, recycled yogurt tubs produce a hard but smooth plastic with a mottled surface color, with just the occasional fleck of authentic silver foil. It is also good to know that each variety of plastic is again recyclable at the end of its life, which makes it a cradle-to-cradle material.

Decorative recycled plastics work well as backsplashes, cabinet doors, bathroom surfaces, and tabletops, but they are not heat resistant and so are inappropriate for kitchen work surfaces.

ECORESIN PANELS

Made from clear plastics—40% of which are recycled—Varia ecoresin panels include a stunning range of wall coverings. The panels are made up in layers, allowing other materials, such as grasses or flowers, to be incorporated.

Ecoresin works wonderfully as backlit wall panels, tabletops, backsplashes and even partition screens. The texture of the natural materials added to the resin provides warmth, yet it is also tough, with almost 40 times the impact resistance of glass. It is also fully recyclable at the end of its life. Currently manufactured only in the United States, ecoresin panels are not so eco-friendly for consumers outside that country, as their transportation entails an increased carbon footprint.

RECYCLED COMPOSITES

There are a number of crushed or recycled material composites that can be used as kitchen

ABOVE A stylized floral-motif wallpaper takes center stage in this homely and highly personal bedroom. A headboard has been dispensed with, leaving just the simple bed, plainly clothed in a patchwork cover of soft, natural shades.

or bathroom surfaces. These composites use small segments of otherwise unusable materials, including stone, glass, and plastics, that are crushed into tiny pieces and then bonded together in a resin (ideally solvent free) to create solid, zero-maintenance surfaces. Not only can these composites be molded to a specific size but additional pieces can be seamlessly joined on during the manufacturing process, allowing chic-looking integral sinks to be added.

Being recycled, these composites have a mottled surface, but they are generally available in a variety of colors. This material has a fresh

sparkle to it since the light catches the particles close to the surface, which contrasts wonderfully with natural materials, such as wood.

TONGUE-AND-GROOVE PANELING
Similar to solid wood flooring, boards for tongue and groove panel come in a range of thicknesses, from about $5/8$ to $1^1/8$ in., and in several different profiles, from a plain style, producing a simple V-shaped groove between each board, to more decorative styles. It is available in many different species of wood: softwood, such as pine, fir, and cedar, as well as hardwood, including cherry and oak. Make sure that any paneling you select comes from an FSC-certified source.

When fitting tongue-and-groove paneling, it is best to leave it in the space to acclimatize and shrink for two weeks prior to fixing in order to prevent gaps from forming. Fit the paneling to a series of studs screwed to the wall at spaces of 16 in., and cut the paneling to fit neatly around any electrical and plumbing fittings.

Many people choose tongue-and-groove paneling for the beauty of the wood itself—its distinctive color, which gives a warm quality to a room, and, in many cases, its interesting grain. The best treatment for such high-quality paneling is to oil it, which protects the wood while allowing it to breathe.

Cheaper paneling may have a less attractive surface; or you may have inherited paneling when buying your house and simply not like it. Here, the sensible option is to paint it. Depending on your chosen color and finish, the possibilities range from the rustic to the subtle and sophisticated. Just be sure to choose a breathable, VOC-free paint.

RECLAIMED LUMBER PANELING
Over the last couple of years I have experimented with paneling walls with reclaimed floorboards. Handled carefully, this treatment can combine a natural material with a contemporary finish. The age and warmth of textured wood imbues any room with atmosphere and adds another visual feature within the space. If you can find aged fencing panels (that have not had bitumen or creosote applied to

them), their silvered finish would look wonderful.

Source wooden floorboards from reclamation yards, and clean them very gently with a wire brush or mild soap and water to retain their character. Wood expands and shrinks, so it is best to let the boards acclimatize to your home for a few days before fitting them onto the walls, using screws and battens. They can then be left natural, oiled, or even dragged with natural paint them to give them a gentle, aged feel.

ECO-WALLPAPER
Environmentally friendly wallpapers are now easy to source in a wide range of decorative designs. Made from 100% FSC-certified lumber or with a high percentage of recycled paper fibers, the paper pulp is made with long fibers so that it withstands wet adhesive and stays strong. The paper is printed with vegetable inks, left to dry and then packaged in biodegradable materials.

Eco-wallpapers harbor no embedded toxins, so this is a healthful product to use in your home. It can be hung using natural starch adhesives and will neither fade nor discolor; the average lifespan of an eco-wallpaper is between five and six years (the time period after which you might wish to redecorate anyway). At the end of its usable life, eco-wallpaper degrades completely, without polluting the environment.

Because these papers have no surface coating, they should not be used in wet areas such as bathrooms or kitchens; however, they are great for use elsewhere. They make for good feature walls and work well when accompanied by a paint scheme that matches the background color of the paper, allowing the pattern to stand out and the paper to blend in.

An alternative is natural wallpapers, which are available in a wide variety of surface finishes, from sisal to sea grass, bamboo to arrowroot. These papers may well have ingredients that have traveled long distances, but they will give a sense of sophistication, natural warmth, and texture to your walls. However, they can be fragile, so are perhaps best kept for areas of low traffic to minimize wear and tear.

ECO-SURFACES

OF ALL THE SURFACES IN THE
HOME, DOUBTLESS THE KITCHEN
AND BATHROOM SURFACES HAVE
THE TOUGHEST ROLES TO PLAY.
THEY HAVE TO COPE WITH
EXTREMES OF TEMPERATURE AS
WELL AS SPILLAGES OF LIQUID,
DETERGENTS, AND FOOD, YET
REMAIN CLEAN AND HYGIENIC.

In addition, surfaces constitute a high percentage cost of any kitchen or bathroom. And being so visible, they form a key part of the look of the space. So when making your choice of material, which has to fulfill so many critical functions, what comes first? Practicality, cost, or style? If choosing the right surface weren't hard enough, I am also asking you to think about the environment when making that decision. As more people reject processed foods in favor of purer produce for health and environmental reasons, it only seems right that the surfaces on which we prepare food reflect this move toward the organic and sustainable. If you are choosing to eat organic and fair-trade, the likelihood is that you are already thinking about eco-issues in the kitchen, so why not also in your design choices?

Alongside looks, durability, and ease of maintenance, place of origin and toxic content (as a constituent part of the material or applied to the material's surface in the form of a finish) must be considered when choosing the perfect surface. Also bear in mind that if you decide to refit your kitchen or bathroom and no longer have a use for the surface, that material must go somewhere. Consider all these issues now.

OPPOSITE Eco-surfaces range from (clockwise from top left): recycled glass, hand-made mosaic, natural slate, crushed and recycled-glass stone, bamboo and recycled plastics.

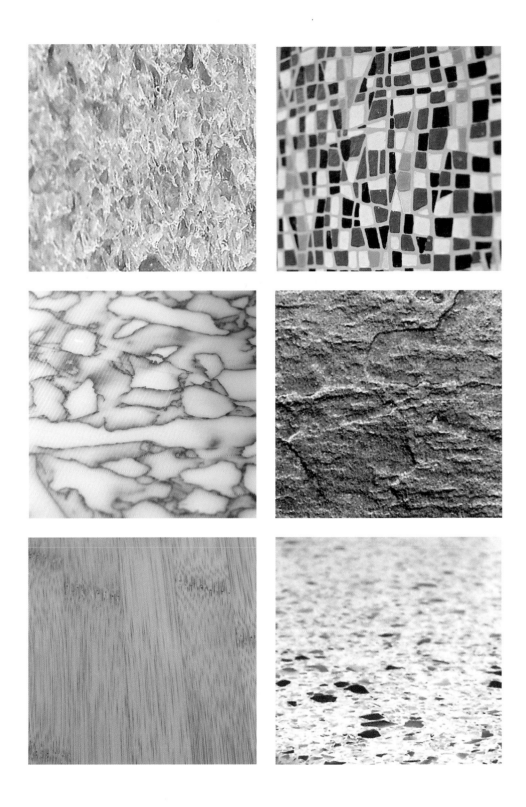

RECYCLED GLASS "STONE"

Various products combine crushed, recycled glass and a liquid binder to form extremely durable, strikingly handsome work surfaces. In the United States, a leading brand of glass stone is Vetrazzo, which contains 85% crushed recycled glass set in a mixture of Portland cement and inert proprietary materials. The mixture is left to cure and harden, then the slab is polished to a silky, high-gloss finish, enhancing the sparkling fragments of glass. Various different colors and color combinations are available. No VOCs are emitted by this material, which is tough, durable and ideal for kitchens, bathrooms, and tabletops.

On the plus side, glass stone is versatile, diverts glass away from landfill, has a high resistance to heat, stains, and scratches, and is low maintenance. On the negative side, all the hard work and time in producing glass stone is reflected in its high cost, similar to that of a natural stone.

Glass stone is an exciting alternative to solid stone or plastic and is available in a dazzling choice of colors. It can either be coordinated with the rest of the kitchen or used to create an impact with intense color. But remember that strong colors are very personal, while lighter surfaces will reflect more light into a space.

DURAT®

Durat® is a man-made material with a high recycled plastics content and is itself 100% recyclable.

Because it is a solid core material—in other words, it is the same material and color all the way through—if it does get scratched or marked, it can simply be sanded back, thereby extending its lifespan in areas of high use. Its downside is that, depending on where you live, Durat® may have a high carbon footprint, as the plastics are collected in Scandinavia, where it is manufactured.

Durat® has a silky finish with a subtle sparkle to it, and is available in an exciting range of colors. The real bonus with Durat® is that lengths of it can be seamlessly welded together, so that you can create as long a section of it as you like. For a professional finish, you can integrate sinks and

basins into the work surfaces, welding the material on and hiding any join lines.

STAINLESS STEEL

Although it may be too harsh for other areas of the home, stainless steel is perfect for the hard-wearing kitchen—it is durable, easy to clean, and light reflective. It also lends an air of the "professional chef" to your kitchen.

Stainless steel can be ordered new and tailored to your space; it needs careful measuring and maybe a template to ensure an exact fit. Its inherent toughness and anticorrosion surface coating means that stainless steel cannot be cut down on site if the wrong size. As a new material, stainless steel contains around 50% recycled material and is itself 100% recyclable, so at the end of its useful life it can be disposed of responsibly.

This high level of durability allows stainless steel freestanding cabinets to be reused again and again. Reclamation yards often have a steady supply of cabinets from professional kitchens ready to be wiped over and reused. Instead of going for the super-sleek (and occasionally characterless) built-in kitchen, opt for freestanding cabinets or even a mixture of both to give your kitchen a freer, funky feel. These pieces contrast wonderfully with natural wood or crisply painted surfaces. At the end of its useful life, you can take it with you, take it back to the yard where it came from, or sell it for scrap.

WOOD

Locally sourced solid wood is the obvious wholesome choice for an eco-kitchen or bathroom. It has a wonderfully warm and tactile surface with a soft directional grain, which makes each piece unique. Wood is hard-wearing and durable and in many respects improves with age. What is more, unlike artificial materials where bacteria are free to reproduce, wood contains natural enzymes that fight unwanted bacteria, which makes it a healthier option for your home.

Because it is not stain resistant, wood needs regular maintenance. Luckily, it can be sanded

ABOVE Bathroom surfaces need to be waterproof, durable, and easy to clean. The natural pebble floor tiles and geometric unglazed wall tiles are softened by the use of the oiled, sustainable oak basin plinth.

RIGHT This glass stone surface is made up of 85% crushed recycled glass in a solvent-free resin, creating a smooth, glossy surface, which sparkles in the sunlight.

ABOVE Stainless steel can be made with a high content of recycled materials and can itself be recycled. The hard lines of this professional-style kitchen are softened by the vintage chairs and open display shelves.

back to remove any marks, thereby having a potentially long lifespan. Ideally wooden surfaces should be oiled or waxed—rather than varnished—once a year to retain their natural feel. Polyurethane varnish simply coats the wood in shiny layers, sabotaging the wood's true quality, and can leak toxins into your home.

If you already have wooden cabinet doors, you should choose a different material for the work surfaces as it can be frustratingly difficult to match the woods precisely, and they will age differently over time. Contrasting materials will break up horizontal and vertical surfaces and set up exciting visual contrasts. Conversely, if you are considering a wooden surface, match it with either glass-fronted or spray-painted cabinet doors.

Whichever wood surface you choose, it is critical that you opt for FSC-certified wood. Then at the end of its useful life the wood can be recycled, becoming a cradle-to-cradle material. It can be either sanded and reused or chipped and then left to biodegrade or used to form wood byproducts, such as particleboard.

BAMBOO
An eco-alternative to large sections of wood is bamboo (see also page 57). Once cut and harvested, small sections of bamboo are laminated together to create solid work surface-size boards.

Bamboo has a natural antibacterial quality, which is a useful property for a work surface. It is naturally light brown, but can be stained or simply finished with a Danish oil to protect it from wear and tear while retaining the material's natural texture and warmth. The drawback to this material is that most bamboo is grown in the Far East; so it can have a high embodied energy due to the distance it must be transported.

NATURAL STONE
Again the main eco-issue with stone is that it is extremely heavy and often must travel far, thereby massively adding to its carbon footprint (see also page 58). The only true eco-option is to avoid stone altogether, unless it is sourced from your own country and, ideally, locally.

Often stone is polished to a sleek, high gloss finish, but I find this can give it a cheap plastic quality, which diminishes the stone's natural texture. Instead opt for a honed (soft sheen) finish, which will keep the stone's wonderful tactile quality. Stone surfaces will need to be sealed before use, so check that the sealant does not contain VOCs or other toxins that can off-gas into your kitchen.

RECYCLED WOOD
A trip to your local reclamation yard can yield some exciting discoveries. And although you must rely on chance, if you are persistent, real gems do turn up. Reclaimed oak or teak tabletops and science lab desks from schools and universities can often be sourced, providing tough, durable surfaces with lots of character. They can be sanded down, or cleaned up or in some cases just left as they are—the wear and tear adding character to the final design.

MOSAICS
Making use of small or chipped fragments of glass or ceramics, mosaics incorporate what otherwise might be regarded as waste materials. Used simply, mosaics can make a patchwork effect, but in the hands of a patient master, they can form astonishing patterns.

Small tiles can be used, but for the serious recycler, fragments of pottery or glass make excellent mosaic materials. These will need to be firmly adhered to a solid backing board before being grouted and polished. This task is not to be taken lightly; if you are considering a mosaic, start with a small surface, such as a tabletop, before attempting larger projects. Although laborious, creating a mosaic surface is a satisfying task. Picture the end result and persevere—it is worth the wait.

ECO-FABRICS

CONSIDER AN INTERIOR AS A SERIES OF LAYERS, BEGINNING WITH HARD, DURABLE SURFACES SUCH AS FLOORS AND WALLS, MOVING ON THROUGH FURNITURE, AND FINISHING WITH FABRICS AND SOFT FURNISHINGS. IT IS THE CAREFUL CONSIDERATION OF ALL OF THESE LAYERS THAT MAKES A WELL-BALANCED AND ECO-CONSCIOUS HOME.

As a tactile, decorative, and insulating layer, fabrics play an important role in every interior. Besides adding color, pattern, and texture, fabrics can also reduce heat loss from a room when used to cover windows.

However, it is important to remember that the production of fabrics makes an enormous environmental impact; the quantities of insecticides and pesticides used in the manufacture of even "natural" materials, such as cotton, not to mention the water consumed, are quite staggering. Furthermore, many fabrics will have been exposed to toxins, such as pesticides, and perhaps coated in stain inhibitors or fire retardants. If this is the case, fabrics can bring toxins directly into your home, creating an unintended level of internal pollution within your living space.

The environmental impact of certain fabrics—for example, wool—can be lower than others. Likewise, as technology progresses, alternative manufacturing processes are being developed that will allow traditional fabrics to be created in more eco-friendly ways.

OPPOSITE Eco fabrics can bring a richness to any interior using (clockwise from top left) cushions made from recycled seat belts, a natural wool felt floor rug, recycled vintage cottons, organic linen bedcovers, an organic wool throw, and an organic alpaca cushion.

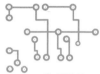

● FELT

For thousands of years, felt has been produced using one of the simplest manufacturing processes—one that can even be practiced on a small scale at home. Felt is a nonwoven textile that relies on the small scales of wool fibers (which expand when wet) to bind it together. Although it can be made using reclaimed fabric, historically felt is made using pure wool, and so its properties and colors can reflect the breed from which it was cut—some being hairier and coarser, while others, such as those made from merino, are softer. Generally felt is made by wetting and then compressing the wool, but it can also be heated with steam to help the fibers swell and interlock.

Being made from wool, felt is a sustainable material that is inherently biodegradable. It is also breathable and, due to its density, extremely warm, while retaining all of the characteristics of wool, including stain resistance and flame retardation. It is a great material to work with, since it does not fray when cut, does not crease too readily, and has good insulation qualities. So it works well when used as a flat-panel window covering. I love the visual weight and density of felt, which can be useful in absorbing noise in echoey rooms.

● INGEO POLYMERS

Ingeo is made using an annually replenishable base material, such as corn, which is processed to produce sugar from the plant starches. This sugar is then fermented to produce a high-performance polymer, from which Ingeo is extruded. With a natural material as its base, Ingeo is itself totally biodegradable under the right conditions.

Ingeo was invented some years ago but had previously been considered too expensive to produce in oil-rich countries, compared to petroleum-based fabrics such as nylon. As the price of oil has risen—making fabrics such as nylon more expensive—so fibers and materials with a natural base have once more become economically viable. As a processed fabric, Ingeo has a higher embodied energy than a fully natural one, but less so than a petrochemical-based fabric.

There are also eco-concerns over the use of land for growing crops for textiles, rather than for food.

As a fabric, Ingeo has a variety of different forms and uses. Its benefits include being stain resistant; having low flammability, excellent UV stability, moisture management, and low odor retention; and being hypoallergenic. Its fibers can be made in different thicknesses, and so it is possible to make it into a variety of different products, from bed linens, throws, and pillows to upholstery, carpet, wall coverings, and draperies.

● LYOCELL

Lyocell is a man-made fiber created from the natural cellulose found in wood, which makes it a sustainable and 100% biodegradable material. Lyocell is made by first dissolving recycled paper with a solvent; the product is then recovered and recycled. The solvent breaks down the fibers of the paper, which are then reformed as it is passed through a series of tiny holes to create a thread.

Lyocell fabric is very strong (more so than cotton) and does not shrink or stretch; however, it does not take color well, so dyes have to be stronger. It also has a tendency to pill after time; but, since it is made of recycled paper, you should not be too hard on it.

In the near future, Lyocell may take the place of viscose and polyester (both petrochemical based fabrics) and possibly even cotton, which uses vast quantities of land, water, and chemicals to produce. Lyocell is currently used for clothing, bed linens, pillows, and quilts.

OPPOSITE This careful arrangement of vintage fabric cushions brings an element of playfulness to a pure white interior space. This final layer of vintage creates a homely balance with the technological and natural elements of the living room.

ORGANIC COTTON

Cotton is one of the world's most ubiquitous materials, used in everything from clothes to curtains, towels to bed linens. It is made from the soft cellulose fiber that contains the seeds of the cotton plant; the seeds are removed and the fibers spun into a thread to make textiles. Cotton accounts for only around 5% of all the cultivated land in the world, but the problem with conventional cotton production is that it also accounts for 25% of the world's pesticide usage. Because it is not an edible crop, much stronger chemicals are used to protect the valuable cotton from predators. This results in a whole host of contamination issues for the local flora and fauna, as well as for those workers who tend the crops.

By comparison, the increasingly wider cropping of organic cotton has combated many of the issues surrounding conventional production. Organic fertilizers are used, while natural pest management has reduced the need for pesticides. To protect those working in cotton production, fair-trade methods have been set up and are carefully monitored from the plant's growth through the fabric's production. This ensures that farmers (many of whom live in developing countries in vulnerable positions at the bottom of the supply chain) are paid a fixed fee—or market price, if that is higher—and so guarantees them better standards of living and working conditions.

Organic cotton is now being used to produce a range of products, from clothes to dish towels and even bed linens. So if you are thinking about using cotton products, make sure that they are made from fair-trade organic cotton. Although it may be a little more expensive, you will have the assurance that neither the environment nor the lives of those producing it have been compromised.

ABOVE Flowing fine linen curtains add a romantic quality to this bedroom. The fabric filters the soft natural light, whilst offering an element of privacy.

ORGANIC WOOL

Few of us realize the fundamental importance of using organic wool for the health of both ourselves and the environment. Organic-wool sheep are reared on land free from potentially toxic chemicals, such as pesticides, and are never dipped; instead, they are bred to be naturally resistant to parasites. Once sheared, the wool (which can be greasy with lanolin) is scoured with biodegradable cleansers, before being carded and spun in a mill—the whole time being kept separate from "contaminated" wool. To further avoid chemicals, heavy metals, and processes, organic-wool products are often used undyed, ranging from natural creams to grays, browns, and black. This not only keeps the wool toxin free but extends this benefit to the land, air, water, and those who work in the industry; the impact really is huge.

There are 8,000 known chemicals in use within the textile industry; choosing organic wool will help to keep your home free from many of these. Often those thought to be allergic to wool are instead suffering reactions to the chemicals used to treat it, rather than to the wool itself.

Elsewhere in the home, wool's natural insulation and fire-retardant properties make it ideal for use as attic insulation. Because wool is breathable and can hold water, it acts not only to keep your home insulated (even when damp) but also to keep it cool in the heat; as the temperature outside rises, moisture evaporates, so drawing heat from the building and cooling it. Wool attic insulation costs a little more; but for my own home, I prefer to be able to venture up into the attic space without getting covered in those tiny shards that come off glass-fiber insulation.

ALPACA

The fiber of the alpaca is amazingly warm and luxurious, but also stronger and lighter than wool. Alpaca has a velvety softness; its hollow fibers make it very warm, and so it is perfect for weaving into blankets or throws.

Similar to llamas, although a little smaller, alpacas are hand reared, largely in South America—Peru, Chile, and Bolivia—by modest farmers who shear and sell their fleece. There are very few of these animals; alpacas are not farmed intensively, which makes their fiber a sustainable product. Although this labor-intensive form of rearing makes alpaca fiber more costly, it does mean that it is less vulnerable to heavily mechanized or chemical production methods, creating a lower embodied energy and a smaller environmental impact. Because alpaca does not contain lanolin, it need not be scoured with chemical cleaning agents and so can be more gently processed. Unlike most other textile products, its embodied energy is related mostly to transportation, rather than manufacture.

Due to the variety of natural alpaca colors—there are up to 22 different shades, from creams to browns, grays to blacks, and even rose—it is less likely to be dyed when being made into products, so reducing its impact further.

LINEN

Made from flax, linen is highly sustainable since the whole plant can be used. While the finer fibers are put to making linen, other parts are used to make linseed oil, livestock feed, and even paper money— so waste is minimized. Once cut and separated from the woody parts of the plant, the long, fine fibers are spun into a yarn and then woven into linen. Known as retting, this process can be carried out naturally or be done chemically, which produces detrimental environmental byproducts. When buying linen, ask how it has been manufactured.

Because linen is breathable, it adjusts easily to body temperature, which makes it a good material for humid conditions—perfect for summer bedclothes. It also has a neutral pH, so is good for those who suffer from sensitive skin or conditions such as eczema. Linen's high absorbency makes it ideal for towels, tablecloths, and bed linens. It is easily washed at low temperatures—good for energy saving—and softens with age but without pilling. It does, however, have poor elasticity. This makes it crease easily. I think this just adds to the fabric's character, but it does make linen a little more labor intensive to use.

HEMP

Hemp is set for a major comeback, due to its many environmental benefits. Industrial varieties are being grown with zero-THC content (tetrahydrocannabinol—the active chemical in cannabis), kick-starting its production on a wider scale.

As with linen, the entire hemp plant can be put to use. It is used to create foodstuffs, fabrics, papers, body-care products, insulation, and oil. Hemp grows in plantations with very little or no need for the use of pesticides and is very fast growing, soaking up a relatively high level of CO_2 and so reducing its environmental impact. For textiles, the stalk is cut, milled, and then turned into yarn.

Hemp is a breathable fabric, and although it is often sold in naturally muted colors, its porous fibers easily take dyes. Hemp fabric can soften with use but remains hard-wearing, and of high tensile strength. It has good resistance to mold and strong UV protection and is naturally fire retardant.

Hemp is commonly used instead of cotton in clothing, carpets, insulation materials, and much more. As a fabric it is coarser than cotton in its raw form—similar to linen in appearance—but now a number of designers are mixing it with other fibers, such as silk, to produce high-end fabrics. Extracting the fibers is labor intensive, which makes hemp time consuming and uneconomic to produce in many developed countries, but feasible in Eastern Europe and China, where people power is still in force. However there is a lot of research being carried out to find ways to change this, so watch this space.

RECYCLED TEXTILES

Reusing fabric is beneficial in a number of ways. It increases the life span of a fabric, reduces its embodied energy, minimizes landfill, and can help you to lower the level of toxins in your home. On top of all that, it means you will not be buying new man-made fabrics and will thereby be lowering the demand for pesticides, fire retardants, and other chemicals used in the textile industry. And by eschewing high-energy manufacturing methods you avoid increasing your carbon footprint.

You can find reclaimed fabrics in a variety of locations, including markets and antique stores, thrift shops, and online auction sites. While you may not be able to find exactly what you want, it can open up a whole new creative design process—so long as you are open to the possibilities of what "textile tapestries" can do for your home, by complementing or contrasting in pattern and color. Using vintage fabrics can add richness to an interior scheme, often setting up an exciting contrast with other, more contemporary features.

Although you could use the fabrics as you find them—stitching pieces together can create wonderful patchwork curtains, cushions, and covers for chairs—if the colors are not right, you could, instead, dye them to match your interior scheme. There is a real art to creating the perfect patchwork, and it helps to have a good eye for color and texture.

Because many vintage fabrics were produced before the introduction of fire retardants, or they may have off-gassed already, there is less chance that you will be bringing toxins into the home. That said, you may want to have vintage fabrics properly cleaned before using them.

ABOVE Crisp white bed linens combined with retro accessories and a vintage patchwork bedspread lend a familiar, nostalgic feel to this attic bedroom.

LEFT Without feeling cloying, the combination of vintage fabrics and patterned knits creates a sense of fun and lends character to this bedroom.

ECO-LIGHTING

GOOD LIGHTING IS ESSENTIAL IF A HOME IS TO HAVE THE FLEXIBILITY DEMANDED BY CONTEMPORARY LIVING. ADEQUATE ILLUMINATION MAKES A HOME SAFE AND EASY TO USE, SATISFYING TO WORK IN, AND INVIGORATING. BY CONTRAST, IT CAN ALSO HELP A SPACE TO BE RELAXING OR EVEN ROMANTIC AFTER A LONG DAY AT WORK.

Having said that, we all need to reduce our carbon footprints by lowering our energy usage —and lighting is a significant area where cutbacks can be made fairly simply. Considering that lighting accounts for on average 15% of the energy we consume in our homes, this is an important area to tackle.

First and foremost, we need to maximize our use of natural light in every area of the home. This can be done through a combination of three actions: allowing as much natural light into a space as possible (without leading to overheating), using reflective surfaces to bounce light around, and choosing a color scheme that throws light back into your space.

But when the sun goes down and the artifical lights must go on, it is essential that the lighting you do have be practical yet use as little energy as possible. Low-energy lighting products are being developed at a phenomenal rate, so gone are the days when you had to compromise on your lighting plan to reduce your energy usage. With the new types of lighting now available, ingenuity and imagination are still needed to create the perfectly lit, low environmental impact space.

OPPOSITE Eco-friendly, low-energy lighting need never be dull, just exercise a little imagination (clockwise from top left): portable, rechargeable eco-lights, a recycled-teacup chandelier, a low-energy bulb in a design-classic swingarm lamp, a reclaimed jelly mold transformed into a lampshade, low-energy Christmas lights attached to branches, and natural wool felt lampshades that stay cool next to energy-saving lighbulbs.

● COMPACT FLUORESCENT LIGHTBULBS

Compact fluorescent lightbulbs (CFLs) are perhaps the best way for us all to reduce our carbon footprint with little hassle or cost. They last up to ten times longer than conventional lightbulbs and over that lifespan use around one quarter of the energy. In fact, that is up to 10,000 hours instead of 1,000 hours and around 15 watts instead of an equivalent 60 watts of energy. Bearing in mind that the average household has around 15 lights, if every lightbulb were changed from incandescents to CFLs, this would add up to a massive saving in both energy use and carbon emissions, not to mention financial savings for you.

However, CFLs do have a few associated problems. They take a little time to reach their optimum brightness; so they are not ideal for use in a hallway, for example, where your need for light may have passed by the time they are fully functioning. Added to which, CFLs do not like to be turned on and off frequently, so they cannot be used with some automatic timer switches. When CFLs finally expire, they must be disposed of properly since each bulb contains a small amount of mercury, which can be recovered. If the mercury goes into landfill, there is a possibility that it might contaminate, but many local authorities are not yet set up to deal with this recycling issue.

Technology in this area is moving fast, and CFLs are consistently improving. They are now available in different shades—soft white generally works best for homes—and their elements are being encased in rubber-coated frosted glass, so they are beginning to look more like conventional incandescent lightbulbs. CFLs bearing Energy Star certification start within one second and do not flicker.

Furthermore, CFLs can now even be dimmed, which makes them more flexible. CFLs are available in a selection of shapes and sizes to suit every light fixture—from the conventional bulb shape to candle bulbs, miniature bulbs, and now even as substitutes for halogen spotlights, known as GU10s.

If you are averse to the appearance of CFLs, but feel you ought to use them, conceal them with a large lampshade—perhaps one made of felt or paper, since they emit so little heat. Or use a number of small ones in an intricate chandelier.

● LIGHT-EMITTING DIODES

Without doubt, light-emitting diodes (LEDs) are the lighting of the future; if you are not using them now, you will soon. If you ride a bicycle, the chances are you are already taking advantage of LEDs with your night lights. Compared even to CFLs, LEDs are incredibly efficient, lasting for up to 100,000 hours and using a fraction of the energy. They are available in a wide variety of colors and, when carefully controlled, can be blended to create spectacular atmospheric effects.

LEDs are available in a number of shapes, but at the moment they are predominantly used in the form of small spotlights, similar in size and shape to conventional halogen lights. In this form, a number of LEDs are grouped together to cast light out in a narrow beam. If you want to use LEDs to provide general illumination for an entire room, you will need an even spread of these lights across the ceiling. Alternatively, LEDs are perhaps best used as task lights, throwing lighting on areas of specific activity in the home, such as a kitchen work surface.

Otherwise, LEDs can create mood-enhancing illumination, either through small portable lights that change color or as downlighters casting colored hues onto walls. However, in order to do this, you will need a transformer and a color-control mechanism, so it is best to speak to an experienced retailer or electrician.

● HALOGENS

Within these lights, electricity is passed through a filament, which is surrounded by halogen gas. Similar to traditional lightbulbs, halogens produce a lot of heat; this is inefficient, as it is energy that could otherwise be converted into light. It is also a frequent misconception that low voltage means low energy—it does not. Halogens simply run on different voltages and so need transformers. In fact, halogens have a lifespan of around 3,000 hours but still use twice the energy of CFLs and

ABOVE Color-changing LEDs can be used to create atmosphere. However, they are best used in a subtle manner, within a small palette of shades to match your interior scheme.

ECO-LIGHTING   87

Vintage lighting can discretely conceal low-energy lightbulbs. This cool combination of romantic crystal chandelier and retro chrome side light creates a functional but irreverent feel to the space.

considerably more than their LED equivalents.

Originally intended as spotlights, halogens are now used for general lighting and liberally perforate ceilings, especially in bathrooms and kitchens. In my opinion, the quality of light produced by halogens is harsh and full of glare. Halogens are also expensive, and since they need changing fairly frequently, they tend to be an expensive way to light a space.

However it is not all bad news. If your home is full of halogen light fittings, the bulbs can be refitted with CFL or, even better, LED replacements, leading to massive savings in energy and cost—not to mention ladder time.

● FLUORESCENT TUBES

Despite their poor reputation, gained through their association with soulless office spaces, fluorescent tube lights perform well in providing an even spread of light across a surface, emitting around four times more light for the energy they consume than conventional tungsten lightbulbs. Fluorescent tube lights work in a similar way to CFLs—electricity runs through a gas to create light. Fluorescent tubes do not produce much heat, instead converting most of the electricity used into light, so are very efficient and can last for between 10,000 and 20,000 hours. They are available in different colors, allowing you to use warmer tones in the home than might be appropriate within a commercial space.

The trick with fluorescent tubes is to conceal them; this will cut down on any irritating glare and ensure that the tube cannot be seen at all, just the glow of reflected light. This can be done by running them along the top of eye-level cabinets in the kitchen or elsewhere in the home to bounce light off a white ceiling. I love to experiment with these lights; the results can be surprising and give a space a real glow.

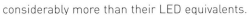 CANDLES

There are inherent dangers in using candles, but when carefully managed and not left unattended, they produce a beautiful, romantic form of light. Candlelight has a soft, warm glow, a gentle, charismatic flicker; and when positioned on a table at eye level in a candelabra, they light faces evenly, with no harsh shadows.

Even candles have an environmental impact, however, so it is worth knowing that some candles are more eco-friendly than others. Conventional paraffin wax candles are most common and easy to buy, but they release a black smoke and soot when burned. This soot, which will blacken ceilings, walls, and fabrics over time, actually contains eleven known toxins, of which two are carcinogenic (toluene and benzene).

The alternatives to paraffin wax candles are palm wax or soy candles, which are cleaner and whiter burning. Palm wax is derived from the fruit of the palm oil tree, which is grown in tropical areas and is used largely in foods, toiletries, and cosmetics. It is important to check that the palm oil comes from a well-managed, sustainable source, which will not contribute to the destruction of tropical rainforests, wildlife habitats, or communities; the governing body of this industry is the Roundtable on Sustainable Palm Oil (RSPO).

Equally, when buying soy oil candles, it is important to make sure they are made with 100% natural ingredients and essential oils, not from a GM source of soy or adulterated with man-made chemicals or fragrances.

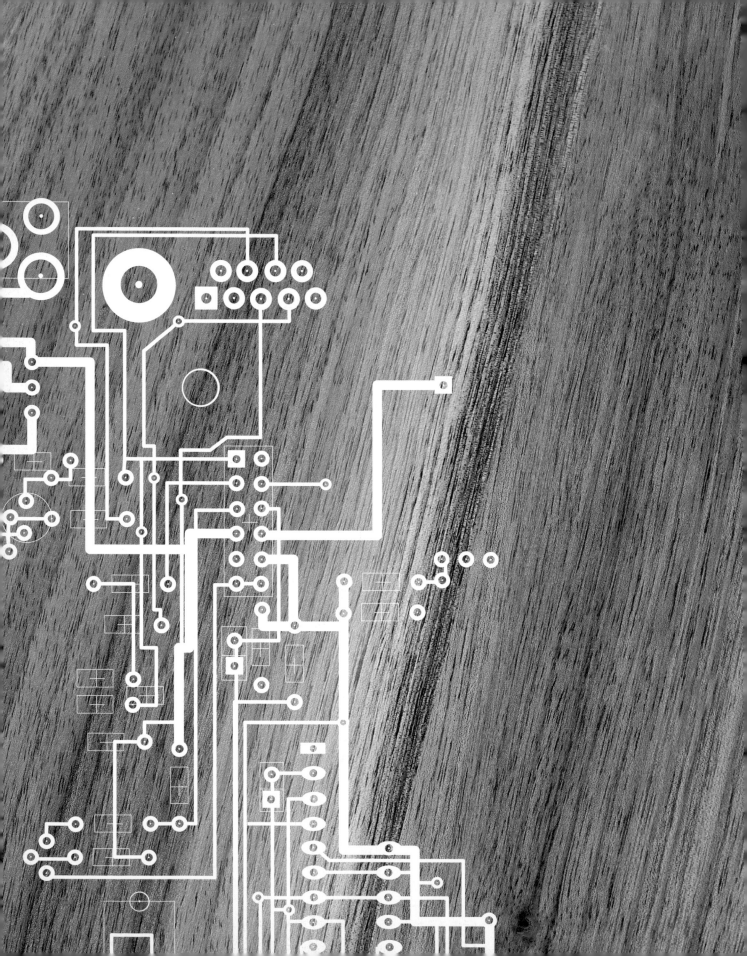

IN THE HOME

KITCHENS AND DINING ROOMS

IT IS WITHIN THE KITCHEN THAT WE USE THE MOST RESOURCES; A HIGH PROPORTION OF THE WATER, ELECTRICITY, AND GAS WE CONSUME ARE FED INTO THIS SPACE. BE LESS WASTEFUL AND MAKE SURE THAT EVERY QUART, WATT, AND CUBIC FOOT ARE USED IN THE MOST EFFICIENT WAY POSSIBLE.

Similarly, a large proportion of the packaging and food we consume on a daily basis finds its way into the kitchen, so the opportunity to recycle and compost is also present. Anyone who is serious about cutting their carbon footprint must focus their thoughts on the kitchen.

When thinking about your kitchen, consider the impact of its entire life cycle—from how it is manufactured, through its everyday use, to what will happen to it once it has reached the end of its useful life. On top of these practical concerns, the kitchen is a major investment; so it should also be durable, cost effective, and ultimately a selling point for your home. In short, the design of the perfect eco-kitchen has to fulfill all these criteria—not forgetting that it is the heart of the home, so it needs to be a welcoming and a pleasurable space to be in.

ABOVE A decidedly vintage kitchen. Instead of wastefully ripping out these retro cabinets, the owner has given them a new lease on life with a coat of warm cream paint. The homely feel that such vintage cabinets lend a kitchen is accentuated by the casual arrangements of personal objects.

ECO-KITCHEN PLANNING

Planning an environmentally friendly kitchen is much like planning a conventional kitchen, except to be truly eco, a kitchen must be built from materials chosen from a specific eco-friendly palette: all appliances must be Energy Star rated, and within the layout adequate space for waste recycling must be incorporated. Obviously, maximizing available space and light and creating an efficient layout will make your kitchen lower-impact and easier to use, thereby giving it a longer life span, but in the kitchen it is also important to remember the green mantra of the 3 Rs: reduce, reuse, and recycle (see pages 14–16).

When planning an urban eco-chic kitchen, you will need to focus on anything that allows you to reduce the amount of resources the kitchen needs in both its construction and its daily use. Look for ways to cut water, electricity, and gas or oil usage—you will reap the rewards in time. Likewise, if you can reuse old items or use sustainably produced materials in your design, it will help you to cut the environmental footprint of your kitchen. Ask yourself whether you really need to rip out the entire existing kitchen to install a new one, or could you simply replace certain elements to give it a whole new feel? If so, you could look to replace only the work surfaces, backsplashes, and door handles while covering or painting the old doors—it really can make a dramatic difference.

Using naturally produced materials will help to cut the level of toxins present. From a personal health perspective, because the kitchen is a place of food preparation, it makes sense to cut down on the use of toxic materials and those that off-gas over longer periods of time within this space.

Although recycling kitchen waste is something we are all now familiar with, it rests at the bottom of the 3 Rs hierarchy; for ideally, you will cut down on what is thrown away in the first place. But also look to use recycled materials in your kitchen's construction, and allow adequate space for recycling packaging and foodstuffs within its design. As recycling processes improve and it becomes possible to recycle more and more materials, so we will need additional storage space in our kitchens—future-proof your home now.

TECHNOLOGY, NATURE, VINTAGE

The cornerstones of urban eco-chic come into their own in the kitchen—a space that combines high resources usage, functionality, and style. Technology provides beautiful cutting-edge low-impact materials, which can be incorporated into a room, and allows appliances to cut down on the amount of resources needed to fuel a kitchen—from dishwashers that use less water than washing dishes by hand to low-energy lights that will last for years and can even be programmed to change color.

The inclusion of nature can create exciting textural contrasts between surfaces and appliances within a kitchen. Besides reducing the level of toxins present, natural materials, such as wood, often improve with age, picking up a rich patina with prolonged use. Natural materials are also easier to recycle at the end of their life, beause they can simply biodegrade.

Incorporating vintage items in the kitchen may add a sense of character to a space that can all too easily be shiny, pristine, and soulless. Whether it is a collection of mismatched chairs, an aged sideboard, or an antique glass-fronted display cabinet, vintage pieces provide warmth and comfort within a home.

KITCHEN CARCASSES

The carcasses of many kitchen cabinets are made from particleboard, which is then covered with a melamine surface finish. In eco-terms, this can be both good and bad: on the one hand, there is a high recycled content in these boards, which is good, but if they contain fomaldehyde they may off-gas toxins, which is bad. Sadly, particleboard carcasses are not very durable. Incredibly, particleboard is not waterproof, so if you have a leaky faucet or a flood, your cabinets can be ruined; so they have only a limited life span and are difficult to recycle at the end of their useful life. Whenever possible, it makes sense to reuse old particleboard carcasses that may no longer off-gas toxins. More durable carcasses are made from plywood or medium density fiberboard, and it is now possible to obtain carcasses made of formaldehyde-free versions of these materials. Look for the label "ZF [zero-formaldehyde] MDF"; and remember, if choosing plywood, to make sure it's FSC-certified.

KITCHEN CABINET DOORS

As a vertical plane, doors play a significant part in the look of your kitchen units. Use them to inject color, a sense of nature, or period style. Whatever you do, make sure they have no adverse effect on your health or the environment.

From a functional point of view, the material should be easy to clean, resistant to scratches, and sufficiently strong to allow for proper fixing. When fixing hinges to doors make sure the material is at least 3/4 in. thick.

There are a number of materials for cabinet doors. The technology option will create a sleek contemporary finish. The nature option—one of the many available species of wood—will give a feeling of natural warmth and texture, as well as long-term durability. Although it may require more work, the vintage option is likely be the cheapest of the three and have a more characterful feel.

TECHNOLOGY

⊙ ZF-MDF panels—these can be cut, routed, decorated, or simply painted, much like conventional MDF.

⊙ Recycled plastic sheets—these come in an array of colors and styles, so choose one that will complement the rest of your kitchen.

⊙ Multi-application recycled plastic sheeting—these are created from recycled detergent bottles, cellphones, and even Wellington boots. Use the sleek whites or slick blacks, but stay away from the multicolored panels.

⊙ Melamine-faced particleboard—although bonded by resin glues with the potential to off-gas toxins, these boards can be made of up to 70% post-consumer wood fibers from pallets and fruit crates, so they have a recycled content of materials that otherwise end up in landfill. However, once damaged they cannot be repaired, so have a lower durability rating.

NATURE

🍂 Solid wood doors—these are often given surface interest with recessed or raised panels. The panels themselves can be grooved or otherwise embellished. Veneers are often used for raised panels.

🍂 Plywood panels—fixed onto sliding rails, the front face of the plywood can be veneered with a thin layer of another type of wood or alternatively left natural or stained.

VINTAGE

❀ Reclaimed wood—these materials, including wire-brushed or painted floorboards, can be made into panel doors.

❀ Fabric hanging panels—fixed onto a cable, these panels can be slid from side to side.

❀ Old sail fabric—fixed onto a hook system, this fabric can look great if sewn carefully so the nautical numbers and symbols show.

KITCHEN SINKS

Any trip to a reclamation yard acts as a reminder that a kitchen is rarely for life. Many kitchens have a lifespan of only 10–12 years. It is worth remembering this when choosing fixtures and fittings, including sinks. Some materials, such as Durat® recycled plastics, can have sinks seamlessly welded to the work surface, creating a sleek, professional look (see page 72). This can be in the same color as the work surface or a contrasting hue for variation; either way it is a good water tight design method.

Stainless steel sinks are available in a wide variety of shapes, sizes, and costs. The material is enormously durable and easy to maintain, with the added benefit that stainless steel is easy to recycle, so your sink is likely to already contain a percentage of recycled material. If you have a solid core work surface, such as wood, choose an under-mounted style sink, which fixes to the underside of the work surface for a sleeker finish. It is also easier to use, with no surface edges to catch dirt or crumbs or prevent water from draining back into the sink. Salvage yards may also have a selection of disused commercial stainless steel kitchen units with integral sinks—perfect if you aspire to being the "pro" chef of the household.

Alternatively, opt for a traditional fireclay (ceramic) sink. Although they have a high initial embodied energy usage, due to the firing process, they are durable, long lasting, and easy to maintain. Visit your local reclamation yard to seek out heritage-style fireclay sinks, which are perenially popular. They will bring a rustic, farmhouse quality to your kitchen with their simple, practical aesthetic.

KITCHEN FAUCETS

The water flow from a running faucet at standard mains pressure can be upward of $2^1/_2$–3 gallons per minute; ideally, this ought to be reduced to around $1^1/_2$ gallons per minute. A reduction in water usage can be achieved by simply consuming less in the first place—for example, cleaning dishes or vegetables in a dishwashing bowl, rather than in the sink, saving precious gallons every day. But if you are fitting new faucets, choose water-efficient, low-flow models. Bear in mind that a flow rate of any less than $1^1/_2$ gallons per minute feels frustratingly slow when filling a pan or bucket. When selecting a faucet, be sure to check that your choice works at the water pressure flowing to your home. This is measured in pounds per inch, or psi. Your dealer can advise you on this.

For water-aware options consider the following:
● Turn down the flow valves that lead from the water pipes to the faucets. Simple adjustment is all that is needed, but make sure that enough water still flows to activate your water heater. This restricts water usage in a crude way, but will not regulate the flow rate.
● Fit a conventional monoblock faucet with flow regulators fitted into the pipes (hot and cold) below the faucet, as low-flow faucets are not always the most attractive. This keeps the flow at a steady rate of 1–$1^1/_2$ gallons per minute.
● Fit a monoblock faucet with a cartridge that has two flow levels—the first level for a general low-flow rate and a second level, achieved by pushing the lever further, for a faster flow rate.
● If you're buying a new washing machine, get a front-loading model. Front loaders use less water—they also use less energy, because most of this is used to heat the water.

ABOVE There is no reason why you cannot choose the faucets you really want, as long as they are fitted with flow restrictors or aerators to reduce water usage. This spring-mounted, commercial-style, plat-washer faucet provides a functional contrast to the natural lumber cladding and stacks of cream crockery.

LEFT Mixer faucets are a good choice for an eco-kitchen. As they blend the hot and cold together, you can control the water temperature at source and reduce wastage.

◉ Fit a faucet with an aerating head—this gives the impression of a faster flow rate while delivering only 1½ gallons per minute. On some conventional faucets with a threaded end, a simple aerator can be screwed in, but check sizes and dimensions before buying.

❀ Visit your local reclamation yard to seek out the vintage option—faucets are often thrown out in full working condition when a new kitchen is installed. If they need work, they may just require new washers and re-chroming. Vintage faucets do not have a high resale value, so this can make for a good budget option, too. Fit vintage faucets with flow regulators for the ultimate in urban eco-chic style.

ADDITIONAL FAUCETS

In the kitchen you may also want to consider a filtered drinking water faucet, which removes any impurities from the main water supply. This will cut down on the number of plastic drinking water bottles that you have to recycle, as it will provide you with a continuous supply of fresh, filtered water for both cooking and drinking. Some faucets have a built-in tri-flow system, allowing an extra built-in faucet to take water from a carbon filter system straight through the conventional spout. If you are worried about any cross contamination, however, use a separate faucet and spout system.

A more recent development in faucets—and one that is set to become a feature in most kitchens—is the instant-boil faucet. One press of the lever, and right away the water boils through air pressure alone, as opposed to a conventional heating element. This dramatically cuts down on the energy used to boil water, as well as the amount of hot water used; it is easy enough to put the water straight into the cup or pan that you are using with no wasteful surplus.

BACKSPLASHES

Backsplashes are the vertical areas that sit to the rear of your work surfaces, so they have a significant impact on the look of your kitchen. Although they need not be quite as hard-wearing as the work surfaces themselves, their primary function is to act as easy-to-clean surfaces, which prevent liquids from dribbling down the back of the kitchen cabinets, which can in time lead to the growth of unhealthy mold.

The backsplash provides a visual opportunity to add exciting textural detail to your kitchen; but remember that keeping surfaces light and reflective will help to bounce natural light around the space. This vertical plane is highly visible and separates the eye-level cabinets from the work surface. So be careful not to use too many materials in your kitchen's palette—it can lead to a messy, uncoordinated feel.

For suitable backsplash options, consider any of the following:

● Ecoresin panels—there is a great variety of these Ecoresin panels to choose from: clear, colored, or even incorporating other decorative materials, such as flowers or reeds (see page 66). Furthermore, these resin panels are easy to work even when the specified measurements are not quite correct. They can look quite spectacular.

● Extended work surfaces—match the material of the backsplash to your work surface. Whether it is wood, bamboo, or slate, consider extending the kitchen work surface vertically up the wall by 4–8 in. This will keep your kitchen coordinated and unfussy. Paint the surface above the backsplash to match the rest of the kitchen.

● Painted walls—use a VOC-free eggshell or latex flat paint that contains no toxins, as you do not want toxins drifting down onto your food preparation area. Painted walls are not as hard wearing as other backsplash materials, and you will need to fit a quarter-round molding between the work surface and the wall to fill the joint and to stop liquids, but it will simply coordinate the kitchen without any fuss.

● Back-painted glass—large sheets of glass can be ordered with any color you choose. This can be easy to clean and maintain, giving a light, reflective, contemporary feel.

🍂 Mosaic or ceramic tiles—these are easy to fit, as you can minimize cutting, thereby reducing any unnecessary wastage (see page 75). Ideally, source tiles made locally in the country you live in to avoid excess transportation.

🍂 Conventional ceramic or stone tiles—again try to source tiles that have not traveled vast distances (see page 75). These can be refreshed every few years by re-grouting them. Avoid using tile paints to refresh your kitchen, as they can have high toxic VOC contents, which will fall onto your food preparation areas.

❀ Stainless steel—easy to clean, light reflective, and professional looking (see page 75). It is often made from recycled materials and can itself be recycled. You must measure up carefully before ordering, as there is no room to alter its shape once the steel arrives.

❀ Recycled glass tiles—these can be sourced in a variety of back painted colors (as opposed to clear, which would allow you to see the wall behind) which gives them a translucent depth (see page 66). You can be creative with the colors (horizontal stripes work well), but try not to go overboard.

TIPS FOR **REDUCING** KITCHEN WASTE

• If your supermarket uses plastic bags, don't accept them. Instead, buy reusable shopping bags and keep them handy for when you go food shopping. With care, paper bags can be reused.

• If you do accept plastic bags, make sure you reuse them as often as possible.

• Use re-sealable storage boxes wherever possible instead of throwaway freezer bags.

• Reuse aluminum foil whenever you can.

• Buy fruit and vegetable loose, rather than encased in any packaging—this is favored by local greengrocers but less so by supermarkets.

• Recycle organic matter and cardboard in a home compost system.

• Grow as many of your own vegetables as you can.

• Choose products with packaging that can be recycled—those made with more than one material are difficult to separate. Market forces can help change the world.

• Do not buy heavily processed food in its own cooking dish with lots of unnecessary packaging.

• Find out what your local government can recycle, you may be surprised.

• Be creative, rather than throwing items away—for example, use glass jars as votive candle holders in the garden.

KITCHEN RECYCLING

In an ideal world, we would all do more to reduce the amount we buy and subsequently throw away. However, that is not always realistic, or indeed even wholly possible in our consumer world, so we need to incorporate proper facilities for recycling in every kitchen. Yes, recycling can be time-consuming and a bit of a pain, but it is essentially very easy to do. So the best way forward is to embrace it as an essential part of modern-day life. It really will take only a small change in the attitude of us all to make a world of difference. If you need further convincing, visit your local landfill site.

Depending on how much you and your family consume, you may need to devote a surprising amount of space to recycling facilities within your kitchen. The pressure on kitchen space can be reduced by finding alternative storage areas, such as an understairs cavity or a hall closet, for items before they are collected and taken to recycling facilities.

It is likely you will want to and be able to recycle **GLASS • TIN CANS • DRINKS CANS • PAPER • PHONE DIRECTORIES • CARDBOARD • BATTERIES • SOME PLASTIC CONTAINERS • ORGANIC WASTE**

Many of these recyclable items can be unsightly, and so storage for them is often best hidden away. This could be the cupboard area underneath the sink; but, because of the bulk of the sink itself, as well as the drain trap, this space is often not big enough to store all the necessary items or even to position a compartmentalized recycling bin. You may need to find an alternative cupboard or to use a separate dedicated recycling bin.

RECYCLING STORAGE

There are a number of neat folding, sliding, and swing-open compartmentalized recycling bins on the market, which help you sort and store items prior to recycling. Choose whichever one is best suited to your needs and available space. Measure your cupboard or closet, and check that the bin opens sufficiently for you to access every compartment. If there are any obstacles to hassle-free recycling, it easily cuts down the amount you and your family actually recycle. If you have no space storage, choose a free-standing separating bin. My own three-section compartment bin has a flip-up lid, which makes it easy to use even when your hands are full.

If you are finding that cans and bottles take up too much space, use a compactor; this useful gadget will make light work of compressing items for recycling. In addition, you may want to find a way to store all those plastic bags that you have promised yourself to stop collecting. They do really pile up, but can be neatly stored away for future reuse.

Recycling organic waste, such as vegetable peelings, eggshells, and other food scraps, can be an unsightly and unpleasant experience. It is best to get any compostable matter right out of the way into a kitchen caddy with a removable lid, which can then be frequently emptied onto your compost heap or into your curbside collection bin. However, a neater alternative is to under-mount a removable organics bin beneath a hole cut in the kitchen work surface, which is accessed via a neatly fitting lid. The flush surface-mounted fitting has a rubber seal that prevents smells from escaping from beneath the lid. This makes it a neat, integrated,

and easy-to-use option, without creating extra clutter to sit on the kitchen work surface.

There is still some debate about the usefulness of electric in-sink waste disposal units. While they do reduce the amount of organic waste that goes to landfill, they also use up quantities of water and electricity to grind waste matter into an unpleasant sludge that heads down into the sewers, which ultimately has to be dealt with by someone else. If possible, it is better for everyone to use a home compost system or curbside organic waste recycling system.

WALLS

It goes without saying that in a kitchen/dining space you will want to cut the levels of toxins as far as possible. Conventional paints release VOCs over time (see page 65). These colorless gases are heavier than air and, as they fall onto kitchen work surfaces, may attach themselves to food as it is being prepared. There is a real danger of ingesting these VOCs. Cut this out by using natural VOC-free paints or inert materials, such as ceramic tiles, in food preparation areas.

In a dining area, you may want to create a different atmosphere from that in the kitchen. Paint kitchen walls in pale shades to bounce light around the space and keep it feeling fresh. By contrast, you can afford to be a little more adventurous in the dining area. Look to use darker shades of paint, wallpapers and hangings or drapes to create a mood. When both kitchen and dining areas are part of one open-plan space, juxtaposing finishes can work well to subtly zone areas of differing functions.

APPLIANCES

A kitchen is likely to house a number of expensive, energy-hungry electrical items, some of which are difficult to do without. Refrigerators, freezers, ranges, cooktops, and dishwashers are considered by many people to be indispensable. In recent years it has become easy enough to purchase energy- and resource-efficient machines thanks to clear energy efficiency labels. Although more efficient appliances may have a higher initial cost, it is important to consider the long-term impact of a purchased item. Buying higher-

quality items means that you can often expect them to be more durable and have a longer life. Being energy efficient, they will cost you less to run over the entire period of their useful life. For details on Energy Star-rated white goods, visit www.energystar.gov, where you will also find lists of retailers offering these appliances.

Although buying the right energy-efficient item is a good place to start, there are some other basic rules to consider. When planning to buy white goods of any type, it is worth spending time doing some homework before you buy.

Besides studying the manufacturer's specifications, you should also read online reviews by other users and consumer research groups to gain a real understanding of the product's construction, durability, and efficiency. Lastly, remember that the manufacture and transport of electrical items takes an enormous amount of energy and releases a high level of toxins into the environment, placing an impact and embodied energy level onto any new appliance. Buying better and less often is the best way forward.

FRIDGES AND FREEZERS

◉ If you don't do much cooking, consider buying a compact fridge (less than 7.75 cu. ft. capacity); these use 20% less energy than the maximum stipulated by government standards.

◉ Never position a cold appliance, such as a fridge, next to a hot item, such as a dishwasher; the heat will reduce efficiency.

◉ A full freezer is more efficient, so keep it stocked with food or even rolled-up newspaper.

RANGES AND COOKTOPS

◉ Although cooking with gas is considered more efficient, it is a limited, carbon-heavy resource. By contrast, electricity can, of course, come from a renewable energy source such as wind turbines (see pages 38–43).

◉ Cooking with an electric induction cooktop can be up to 74% efficient, compared to 43% for gas. Induction cooktops heat just the base of the ferrous pan with little waste heat spilling out either side. They are also easy to clean and highly controllable, which means that those who use electric induction cooktops to cook love them.

◉ Large-capacity ovens take a long time to heat up, drawing a lot of energy. If possible, have two ovens, one large and one small— perfect for cooking for different numbers.

◉ A conventional oven is less efficient than a convection fan-assisted oven.

◉ A ventilating fan is a necessity to draw away fumes and smells and ventilate cooking areas. Look for energy-efficient models.

◉ A microwave uses less energy to cook food and in less time than a conventional oven, but it can encourage the use of excessively packaged, processed ready meals, as opposed to the eating of freshly prepared foods.

✤ Choose a range made of stainless steel, which can be recycled at its life cycle's end.

DISHWASHERS

◉ It is believed that the most efficient dishwashers may use less water—some manufacturers say up to 80% less—to wash a given number of dishes than required to wash by hand. The machine must be full to capacity.

◉ Dishwashers are available in a variety of different sizes—standard, half-width, and even pull-out drawer versions, so find the one that is right for the number of people in your home.

◉ If your dishwasher is located in a kitchen/dining space, noise from the machine can be a real pain. Inquire how loud your chosen dishwasher is, and compare it to other available models.

◉ Buy a dishwasher with a long guarantee (up to five years), which suggests the manufacturer is confident of the machine's durability.

◉ Some dishwashers can sense how dirty the dishes are (through testing the water during the cycle) and adjust the amount of energy and water used accordingly.

TABLES AND CHAIRS

Along with beds and sofas, the dining table is one of the most significant home furnishings. In my mind, it is the social hub of the home, around which all shared activity centers. When used regularly for meals, it is the one real chance we get to sit face-to-face to interact without distraction. It becomes a vital part of the daily, monthly, and yearly routine— introducing an element of ritual into the lives of those who use it, which will be both grounding and orienting.

Choosing the right dining table is something that you should take time over, ensuring that it is the right style, size, and type for your home. You could opt for a straightforward fixed size and shape table, which will give a sense of stability and structure to the space. If you are pushed for room, a flip-up or fold-out table will still transform your home into a sociable space. Some retailers sell adjustable wall brackets that will support a table for two or fold-out wooden table and chair sets. Alternatively, if the number of people who may sit around the table is likely to vary, or you are into dinner parties, look for an extending table. As with any item of furniture, a table with built-in flexibility represents an environmental saving.

Similarly, the chairs that you choose to go with the table will add to the whole impact of your dining area and can offer a chance to create something really exciting. While many retailers sell matching table and chair sets, this can sometimes look very formal, creating a very set effect. Don't be afraid to mix styles of chairs— add cohesiveness with small details such as soft fabric covers in one color or material.

ABOVE A successful mix of vintage chairs can look less contrived than an entire set in the same style. With vintage furniture becoming increasingly sought after, why not start a collection of key pieces?

DINING TABLES

Remember the urban eco-chic principles of technology, nature, and vintage? Each will impact on the overall style of your dining space in varying ways, creating different looks. The technology options will create a slick, clean, sophisticated feel in your dining space; the nature options will add a sense of wholesome, natural dining with a feeling of solidity and real warmth; and the vintage pieces will add a quirkier, more unusual, characterful feeling to your space making it truly unique.

TECHNOLOGY

● Glass tabletops with fixed or simple trestle table legs—these can allow light to filter through the tabletop to bounce off the floor and up into the room. Glass does have a high embodied energy, through the manufacturing process, but enjoys a classic, enduring style.

● Recycled plastic tabletops mixed with new or vintage bases and legs—these are available in a number of speckled colors and make good surfaces. Some plastics can be overpowering, but those with simple or single shades work well to produce a durable surface.

● Recycled glass stone table tops—crushed recycled glass makes an exciting and sparkling surface (see page 72). It is warm to the touch and very smooth. You can choose the proportions of glass and background cement-resin color to tie in with the rest of the space. This will be a real talking point.

● Plywood tabletops—a number of manufacturers are now making cut-out plywood furniture that has a phenolated (dark brown color) or melamine (often white) surface. This has the advantage of being transported as a flat plywood surface for much of its material life, both to the place of manufacture and to your home, which makes it an efficient and contemporary dining table solution. Other forms of natural plywood can be used, but the top surface can be relatively soft and prone to being easily scratched.

NATURE

🍃 Wood—a solid wooden table will have a visual weight and earthy sense of wholesomeness. It will age well—improving over the years and mellowing in color—acquiring an heirloom quality. Choose one made from FSC-certified wood (see page 57), ideally grown in your own country. Oak, pine, spruce, and beech are good options. Being a solid surface, wood can, if scratched, simply be sanded down to hide any marks. Finish with Danish oil (polymenized linseed) or natural wax to bring out the texture of the grain and warmth of the material.

🍃 Reclaimed teak—tables are being made from teak by a number of manufacturers. The wood, which has a rich red color, is reclaimed from buildings being torn down in the Far East and India, then manufactured into furniture before being shipped. Remember that this furniture will have a higher carbon footprint than any made in your own country. Make sure that your supplier has FSC certifications and follows fair trade practices.

🍃 Bamboo—this multifunctional material is tough and durable (see page 57). Because it grows so fast, it is very reasonably priced. Like many timbers, it has natural antibacterial properties, which makes it good for work surfaces and tabletops. Again, this material is likely to have been manufactured in the Far East, so will have a large carbon footprint.

ABOVE Recycled-glass stone has been used here to create a diner-style kitchen table. Teamed with sleek plywood benches and contemporary plastic chairs, it helps to give this kitchen a high score in eco-friendly technology.

VINTAGE

You don't have to look far to find a vintage wooden table—markets, antique stores, secondhand stores, online auction sites are all great sources for furniture that has a ready-worn, rich patina. These pieces can have a relaxed, distinctly un precious quality, which can make them great for informal family dining. Clean them gently and simply re-oil the wood to retain its true character. Alternatively, you could find a retro glass-topped table that will add an air of character and style to your home. For real style, look for tables from the 1950s and '60s with chromed steel legs.

❧ Reclaimed wood—this can make for an exciting D.I.Y. project. Visit your local lumber reclamation yard and find anything from old scaffold boards and floorboards to slices of real timber that still has the bark on the sides.
❧ Use your imagination and track down a really unusual piece—this could be as simple as an old door or even an industrial table. One of my own favorite tables was made from a reclaimed leather-cutting table, which I then suspended from the ceiling.
❧ Re-cover an old wooden table using mosaic tiles or fragments of pottery—this will create a unique but satisfying piece.

Whilst less efficient in their use of space, free-standing kitchen cabinets create a more relaxed and characterful feel. Here stainless steel, open shelves add to an informal look that contrasts with the natural timber work surfaces and aged wooden floorboards.

KITCHENWARE

If you have gone to the trouble of creating your very own eco-kitchen and dining area, it is a shame to fill it with products that have neither the environmental credentials nor the style to match. Luckily, you can choose from a vast array of beautifully eco-chic kitchenware that has taken its impact into consideration, whether it is low-energy, fair-trade, or from a sustainable or recycled source.

DISHES

It is important for dishes to be durable, so that they can be used over and over again, be put through a dishwasher, or washed in the sink. At the same time, however, since they are used with such frequency, it essential that they complement your table and your food. Luckily, there are several urban eco-chic options:

● Recycled glass—made from crushed recycled bottles, this is often clear with a slight greenish tinge. It is often of high quality, very durable, and, I am glad to say, also very stylish. It is available in a range of styles and sizes and in a number of colors—with a back-painted finish—that can be mixed and matched to add interest to your table. Being dishwasher safe, recycled glass dishes are a durable, long-lasting eco-option for your table.

🍂 Bamboo—plates can be created from this grass in one of two ways. In one method, it is cut into small strips that are wound around a mold then glued together (with a non-toxic glue) to create a pattern of concentric circles. This is then covered with a protective clear lacquer on the inside and optionally decorated with vibrant colors on the exterior. Alternatively, the bamboo fibers are pulped and mixed with a biodegradable resin binder—80% bamboo and

20% resin—to create a dark brown speckled material that is then molded into cups, plates, and bowls. When bamboo crockery reaches the end of its life, it can be composted, rather than sent to landfill.

※ Vintage plates—these are always an option for those on a budget, market lovers, and avid collectors. It is always easy to pick up sets of vintage china and easier still to get hold of individual plates. If you are going for the latter option, my tip is to pick a color, pattern, or style and buy only that to create a cohesive collection—be it a particular shade, a floral pattern, or even a style from a specifc era, such as the 1960s.

GLASSWARE

Since glass bottles are so ubiquitous, the best eco-choice of drinking glass is those made from re-formed, crushed, recycled glass. The styles and designs available are much improved from the early, chunkier options, with the most current designs being slender and elegant. Again, they have a slight greenish tinge to them.

Glasses are also produced directly from reused bottles—the top section is sliced off to create a tumbler from the remaining bottom half. While these were innovative at the time of invention, they now seem rather crude and are, in a way, the first generation of eco products.

Being both durable and endlessly recyclable as a material, stainless steel spun into cups could always be an option. While it has a relatively high embodied energy, its hard wearing quality means that it can be use for years and years. Created and used largely in Asia, stainless steel cups are available mostly as tumblers in ethnic

food stores. They may well complement the style of a table setting, used as water goblets, when mixed with other glassware.

You will also find that markets and secondhand stores are teeming with old glassware, just waiting for someone with a good eye to carefully put sets together. Again, these collections work best when you group together specific sets of glasses such as round wine glasses, small shot glasses, or crystal goblets—their similarity and differences will play off each other wonderfully on your table.

UTENSILS

Utensils may be best made from stainess steel—being so hard wearing and easy to use gives it a long life span. Again, because stainless steel is so recyclable, it often has recycled content. You will also find that, being such an adaptable material, stainless steel is available in a wide variety of designs to suit almost every taste. When you have finally finished with it, you can take it to a thrift shop or metal recycling yard for reprocessing.

For a touch of Old-World glamour, there is an enormous selection of vintage utensils available. As long as you are okay with the idea of others having used it before you (much the same as in any restaurant), this is a great and affordable option. Secondhand cutlery may be silver-plated, have bone handles, or even be in retro 1960s designs. Again, pick your era or style and stick to that for a cohesive look.

STORAGE JARS

Whether for cereals, pasta, oils, or herbs, there is a good variety of storage options open to you made from clear recycled glass. This allows the products that you use to be continually in sight and adds to the style of your kitchen, giving it a more wholesome feel. Made in all shapes and sizes, recycled glass storage jars are robust and easy to use, often having cork lids to keep the contents fresh.

In an effort to reduce the products that you use in the kitchen, instead of wrapping food in aluminum foil or plastic wrap, you might invest in a good selection of reusable polypropylene plastic boxes. These are wonderfully multifunctional—good for use in fridges and freezers and even on picnics—and can easily be recycled once you have finished with them.

COOKING PANS AND UTENSILS

Over the years there have been a number of scares about the materials that we use to cook with and their effect on our health. Aluminum pans were thought to contribute to the onset of Alzheimer's disease, through the ingestion of the metal. However, there has been a vast amount of research carried out on this subject, and current expert thinking is that there is no connection to be concerned about.

However, there is far more conclusive evidence of toxins associated with the use of nonstick pans. Their slippery coating contains substances such as PTFE and PFOA, which are known carcinogens and off-gas toxins when taken to high temperatures. This can happen if a pan boils dry or when frying foods, but is more likely when the surface is worn and scratched.

While these toxins are undetectable by humans, they can be ingested and collect in the body. They are also very dangerous to domesticated birds, who can die within a few minutes of direct contact with the fumes. So not only think twice about keeping your pet parrot in the kitchen, but consider using alternative cookware, such as stainless steel pans and ceramic baking dishes.

You may also wish to reevaluate your cooking utensils, which may be made from PVC-containing thalate plasticizers, which make plastic flexible and bendy. Again, these can be toxic when they degrade through heat and use. Instead use wooden utensils, made from an FSC source, that will not melt, poison you, or scratch the bottom of your pans.

CHOPPING BOARDS

Besides having a wonderful wholesome feel, which is great when you are cooking, many types of wood have good antibacterial qualities; so, from a practical point of view, wood makes excellent chopping boards. With a wide selection for sale, it is worth checking that the wood is sourced from a well-managed sustainable source and is FSC certified. Alternatively, look for newer selections of bamboo chopping boards, which will also have antibacterial qualities, and are likely to be affordable, due the speed of the grasses' growth.

OPPOSITE Keep an open mind to alternative decorating ideas when designing your kitchen; don't be afraid to break with convention. This practical family home utilizes easy-clean, professional freestanding kitchen work tables in conjunction with robust stainless steel carts on casters for storage. The industrial-style light fixtures, along with the sleek gray floor, complete the warehouse feel of the space, which is softened by the warm wood dining table and spots of bright color brought in by the homewares, not to mention the weekly shopping lists scrawled across the chalkboard-painted feature wall.

BATHROOMS

BATHROOMS ARE OFTEN SMALL AND CRAMPED. YET AFTER THE KITCHEN, THE BATHROOM IS WHERE WE USE THE MOST RESOURCES—WATER, HEAT, AND ELECTRICITY. SO DESPITE ITS HUMBLE PROPORTIONS, THIS ROOM HAS A POTENTIALLY EMBARRASSING CARBON FOOTPRINT.

A bathroom is a highly functional space, where all materials used must be durable. Installing a new bathroom can be expensive; but beware of cutting corners, for bathroom fixtures must withstand daily dousings of water, soap, and other cleaning agents. Considering that the average bathroom suite is replaced every eight years, what happens to your old fixtures is crucially important. If you can minimize the items that you must replace, all the better. Try giving your old bathroom a makeover; a fresh coat of paint, clean grout around the tiles, new faucets, a replacement toilet seat, pristine white towels, and the addition of a plant can make a world of difference. If you must tackle a full refurbishment, recycle whatever you can. In addition, remember that a vibrantly colored bathroom suite is a personal choice— one that a prospective house buyer may not share. So opt for classic white to extend your bathroom's appeal and lifespan.

TECHNOLOGY, NATURE, VINTAGE

Due to its highly practical nature, the bathroom relies heavily on technological advances to minimize its use of resources. From a design angle, the bathroom is a private area and one of the more sensory spaces of the home; so nature can also play a key role, offering up sensuous materials to create a spa-like experience in even the most meager of spaces. The materials play an important role in physically stimulating or soothing our bodies; it is where we both refresh ourselves in the mornings and relax after a long day at work. Although the hard working nature of a bathroom offers little opportunity for the introduction of vintage, an old leather armchair nestled into a corner or an ornate wall mirror will go a long way to soften the harder edges of the space and add character.

OPPOSITE For designers, the bathroom is an exciting yet complex space, where function and style must combine; but it is now also essential to exert an environmental consciousness when planning a bathroom. This bathroom feels luxurious but conceals its eco features. From flow-restricting faucets to a generous-sized window, which allows light to flood in, to a handheld shower mixer in the bath that helps to save water. The vintage wicker chair makes this a space to spend time in and relax.

WATER-SAVING DEVICES

Until recently, we have assumed that our access to water is infinite. It is cheap and—in most parts of North America and Europe—plentiful; so why should we care how much we use? With the acceleration of climate change, we are beginning to see massive fluctuations in rainfall, and even some of the soggiest regions are starting to see variations in water availability, through either flooding or drought. Water is predicted to become a scarce resource in the future.

Anticipated water shortages are set to be a global problem, but what can you do at home? Whether you are tackling a complete refit or want to reduce the impact of exisiting fixtures, there are a number of water-saving devices to incorporate into your bathroom. Cutting back your water consumption will save you money and shrink your home's carbon footprint in two ways: by reducing the amount of energy used to heat water as well as the electrical energy needed to pump water to your home in the first place.

LOW-COST WAYS TO SAVE WATER
- Keep your showers under five minutes, and keep baths to a minimum.
- Turn off the faucet while brushing your teeth.
- Fit flow restrictors to faucet valves.
- Fit a water displacement device in your toilet.
- Turn down the temperature on your hot water heater; it is pointless to mix scalding water with cold—this wastes water and fuel.

HIGHER-COST WAYS TO SAVE WATER
- Fit low-flow sink faucets.
- Fit a low-flow showerhead.
- Install a dual-flush toilet.
- Install a gray water recycling system.

LOW-FLOW FAUCETS

Faucets are potentially wasteful devices. Leaving a faucet on while brushing your teeth squanders a minimum of $1^1/_2$ gallons of water per minute, but possibly as much as 3 gallons. Furthermore, a dripping faucet can waste a staggering 1,400 gallons of water over a year; so doing simple repairs like replacing a washer can make significant reductions.

If your faucets are old (installed before the 1992 federal law on water conservation in plumbing), they are probably wasting water. One water-saving tip is to partially close the shut-off valve on each faucet's supply pipe. Get the balance right, and you will barely notice the reduction, yet you will save water and money. If you have a tankless, water-heating system, take care not to turn down the valve to the hot faucet so much that the boiler does not turn on. An alternative is to fit an aerator, which simply screws on to the end of your existing faucet. This mixes the water with the air, giving the impression of the same flow rate. Early models of aerator merely restricted the flow, but newer models incorporate a flow regulator, which, besides preventing a flow of more than $2^1/_2$ gallons per minute (the legal maximum for new faucets) ensures the same flow even if the water pressure drops. Aerators are inexpensive and easy to fit.

However, aerators are not especially attractive objects, so for a more streamlined effect, consider getting a new faucet, which will have an aerator built in. Admittedly, this will entail throwing away the old faucet, but if it is more than 15 years old (predating the water conservation law), it may have become corroded and reached the end of its useful life.

RIGHT Creating a wet room is a sophisticated way to utilize bathroom space that would otherwise feel quite small. Use a flow restrictor or low-flow showerhead system for a luxurious, drenching, yet water-efficient shower.

SHOWERS

As with faucets, showers are subject to federal legislation regarding water flow. Newly installed showerheads must not deliver more than $2\frac{1}{2}$ gallons per minute—as compared to conventional old-style showerheads, which can deliver 4 gallons or more. To convert an old but still usable showerhead into a low-flow version, you can simply fit an aerator to it. Some aerators have several settings and can be used to turn the shower on or off. New showerheads have an aerator built in. They also may contain useful features such as an antiscald valve, which prevents a sudden increase in water temperature caused by someone elsewhere in

the house turning on cold water and diverting it from the mix in the shower. This is well worth having, especially if children use the shower.

In general, taking a shower—assuming a low-flow showerhead—is a more eco-friendly way of washing than taking a bath. A three-minute shower uses less than 8 gallons of water, as compared to about 20 gallons for a bath. But a prolonged shower, or more than one shower a day, will significantly increase your water usage, as well as your energy consumption and your utility bill. To avoid water-wasteful daydreaming, set an egg timer for a frugal few minutes.

TOILETS

It is staggering to think almost 30% of all water used in the home is flushed down the toilet. A toilet installed before 1992 (when a federal law established new water-conservation measures) may use 3$\frac{1}{2}$ gallons or more with every flush. By placing a water displacement device in the cistern, you can reduce this to less than 3 gallons. A low-tech alternative is a brick wrapped in a plastic bag. Both methods reduce the water that flows into the cistern after each flush, while still allowing it to operate efficiently.

Or you could upgrade your toilet, installing one of the newer low-flow models, which comply with the federal law, using only 1.6 gallons per flush. Technology in this area has improved significantly; the early low-flow toilets often required more than one flush, but recent models are fully as efficient as the old wasteful ones. You can also buy dual-flush models (popular in Europe), which give you a choice of less or more water (still within the federal restrictions), depending on the job to be done.

BATHTUBS

It is clear that a bathtub adds value to a property, even if it does conflict with the eco-interior designer's best water-saving intentions. From a quality-of-life perspective, it is difficult to beat a luxurious soak in the bath after a long day. Plus, if you have children, not having a bathtub can make life very difficult. So with this in mind, what is your best option?

Very simply, choosing a small bathtub—perhaps one measuring 66 x 27 in. or even less—over many of the oversized tubs available will instantly lead to a reduction in water usage each time the tub is filled. Because tubs are generally filled to a required level, there is little point in fitting low-flow faucets or flow restrictors. Simply take fewer baths and more showers.

If you have only a limited amount of space, the obvious option is to choose a combined bath and shower in conjunction with a screen. This could simply be a conventional tap with a shower hose attachment and a fabric screen hung from a rail. But if you plan to install a new tub, opt for a fixed-head shower with a flow restrictor and a folding glass screen. Be sure to choose a tub with a reasonable standing area and a flat bottom to reduce the chances of anyone slipping over. A grab bar is a worthwhile accessory, especially if an elderly or infirm person will be using the tub and shower.

When considering style, you may prefer a double-ended tub, with the faucets in the center, which allows two people to bathe comfortably—and with a touch of romance. Otherwise, when making your choice, remember that at the end of its useful life a cast-iron or steel bath can be taken to the scrap metal dealer to be recycled (you will even get a little money back for the former) but an acrylic bathtub is made from a petro-chemical plastic and will only end up in landfill.

Alternatively, you could consider a vintage free-standing bath, which will add a luxurious touch of glamour to your bathroom. These can date from 1880 onwards with the claw-foot bathtub being especially popular. These can be bought from reclamation yards or even online, but be sure to check that the enamel coating is undamaged and that the fitting holes are of a standard diameter. Be warned: some of these cast-iron bathtubs can be extremely heavy; so check the weight and the dimensions of your floor joists before purchase.

GRAY-WATER SYSTEMS

If we were to think carefully about our bathroom water usage, it would seem odd that we allow bath, shower, and sink water to flow away, when it is still perfectly usable for flushing the toilet. There are now a number of systems on the market that recirculate waste water to a storage tank (that holds around 25 gallons), where it is skimmed and filtered before being used in the flushing of the cistern—theoretically reducing your water usage by 30%.

One of the main problems with gray water recycling is the presence of any chemicals, detergents, and dirt in the water. Combined with the fact that it may well be warm, gray water is an ideal breeding ground for bacteria. Gray water needs to be treated with chemicals (which can be environmentally harmful); otherwise it can be kept for only a few days, after which time it will go stale. Also, as the water is contaminated it can only be used in relatively small quantities on garden plants.

In theory, gray water recycling systems make perfect sense. However, in reality it is probable that the costs associated with installing such a system on a domestic scale would outweigh the savings made from the reduction in water usage, making the payback period lengthy.

OPPOSITE LEFT Choosing a small-sized basin is an easy way to reduce water usage. Simply put, a smaller basin means less water is needed every time the basin is filled.

OPPOSITE RIGHT Where space is at a premium, consider a smaller, space-saving toilet, which can be wall hung. Because the dual-flush cistern is concealed and the bowl hovers above the floor, allowing you to see all the way back to the wall, an illusion of greater space is created.

WALLS

Due to the destructive qualities of water and condensation, walls in the bathroom must be scrupulously protected. A cheap quick fix is to coat all surfaces with thick gloss paint, but this will fill the space with high levels of VOCs (see page 65), which off-gas toxic residues and lead to breathing problems and allergic reactions. In addition, paint protects a surface for only a short time before it starts to peel and crack.

A much better solution is to part-tile and part-paint walls. The tiles allow any water to run off quickly, reducing damp levels. Some eco-paints mark when splashed, so a good option is to use a natural eggshell paint that is mark resistant and hard-wearing without the toxic chemicals.

FLOORS

Because of the bathroom's demanding conditions, flooring options are more limited than in other areas. Although bathroom flooring should feel good underfoot, it needs to be hard-wearing, water resistant, and able to deal with variations in moisture content. Additionally it needs to coordinate with the color scheme of your bathroom; it is important visually, whether creating sleek lines or adding a textural finish.

Here are some options:

🍃 Linoleum—waterproof, relatively inexpensive, and extremely hard-wearing, this is available in wide rolls, eliminating the need for seams.

🍃 Cork tiles—although square, these can be cut in half and used to create interesting patterns; they are water repellent.

🍃 Ceramic tiles—hard-wearing and cost effective, although without such good environmental credentials. Cold to the touch, so use with a bathmat or infloor heating.

🍃 Solid wood—susceptible to the changing moisture levels, so apt to swell and contract. Counteract this by fitting expansion cavities under baseboards.

🍃 Rubber tiles—hard-wearing yet soft, with a contemporary look. Available in a selection of surface textures with good anti-slip properties.

🍃 Recycled rubber flooring—available in a roll to create a seamless floor.

LEFT Bathroom design has become an increasingly exciting area in recent years. New materials, such as Ecoresin with encapsulated water reeds, as seen in the wall panels behind this shallow, yet wide, basin, have brought a myriad sensuous textures into what was once a conservative space; it is now possible to create an exotic spa feel within your own home.

OPPOSITE For rooms where space is not an issue, a freestanding bathtub makes a strong design statement. However, a generous tub need not be wasteful when it comes to water usage if a gray-water system recycles spent bathwater into toilet cisterns for flushing.

ABOVE This bathroom combines a small contemporary water-saving basin with a natural, textural, rough-hewn wooden plinth. The candelabra adds a touch of vintage elegance and romance to this sensuous bathing space.

LIGHTING

To create a truly multifunctional space that refreshes you in the morning and relaxes you after an exhausting day, maximize natural light levels and install three types of artificial lighting. All too often, bathrooms have a cool atmosphere, due in part to the large expanse of hard surfaces—tiled floors and walls—which create an echoey environment but also to the wall color and limited light available through what is usually a small window. As with any space maximising the natural light is the key to reducing the environmental impact your bathroom's electricity usage (see pages 16 and 32). Now you may balk at the idea of three types of lighting; but believe me, the effects are worth it. Good lighting design transforms a bathroom from an invigorating space to a calming spa. Good general lights, such as ceiling-mounted spotlights distributed evenly, are essential; task lighting above the sink mirror allows you to see yourself clearly; and lastly, soft mood-enhancing lights create a tranquil space.

GENERAL LIGHTING

Bathrooms are zoned into areas of safety; the nearer the water-bearing item, such as the shower, the higher the safety covering of the light must be to lower the risk of electrocution. As a result, most bathrooms have recessed spotlights, as opposed to ceiling-mounted pendant bulbs. Unless these lights have been recently upgraded, the chances are that they will either be conventional incandescent bulbs or halogen spotlights, both of which have relatively high energy usages and short lives (see pages 84–9). In addition, ceiling-mounted halogen spotlights create a harsh, unflattering light, which increases the shadows under the eyes and the appearance of wrinkles—not good at all as you prepare to leave the house and want to feel your best. If you do have incandescent bulbs, they can now be replaced by long-life, energy-saving fluorescent bulbs, available in a wide range of shapes and sizes—enough to replace all conventional bulb types.

If you have tired of the harsh light and low lifespan of conventional halogen spotlights, you could replace the halogen fittings with LED spotlight fittings and soft white bulbs. Currently these do not have quite the light output of halogens (although this is improving fast), so you may need to add an extra few bulbs to compensate for the lower output. If you specify the correct drivers (like conventional ballasts) and switching mechanisms, they can also be made into dimmable, mood-enhancing lights.

Fluorescent tubes have a reputation for harsh and unforgiving lighting; but if concealed they can give out a useful, even wash of softer reflected light—perfect for general lighting in the bathroom. Conceal them in wall recesses or above built-in cabinets, so that the bulb is not visible, and make sure they cannot be touched.

TASK LIGHTING
Much as in the dressing rooms of actors, task lighting is best placed at eye level around the bathroom mirror, evenly lighting the face, with no harsh shadows. A number of mirrors are now available with built-in top or side lighting, activated by a conventional switch or drawstring pull. These are most likely to be compact fluorescent tubes but may also be single spotlights, which should ideally be low-energy LEDs. Refrain from being too creative

with these lights (it is best to avoid vintage fixtures), as they must be properly concealed in order to protect yourself from electrocution.

ADDITIONAL MOOD LIGHTING
However, if you want to take your lighting a stage further, think about incorporating some fixed low-energy and low light-level fittings. Floor-level recessed wall lights (similar to stair lights) work wonderfully dotted around the perimeter of the bathroom to gently light a space, while permitting you to walk around safely. These will reflect softly off the floor and look great combined with a textured tile or wood floor.

Alternatively, if you have the space, consider a simple domestic LED fiber-optic system fitted into the ceiling above the bathtub. This twinkling light fitting gives the effect of a starry sky at night, soothing away the stresses of the day. Mood lights work well when fitted to a ceiling-mounted infrared sensor, which will detect your movement and switch on the light as you enter the room at night—allowing the lights to operate without forcing you to fumble for the switch or temporarily blinding you as the main lights are switched on. They can simply be set to operate for short periods, so that lights are not left on in the middle of the night.

FURNITURE

If you have the space, some freestanding furniture can transform your bathroom from a functional space to a luxurious one. The addition of a vintage chair will soften the harder edges of the bathroom. You can further soften the effect with a cushion or a throw. Also, of course, a chair can be used to hold clothing or towels while you bathe or shower.

If you do not have space for a big chair, why not consider finding a low stool or even a small old folding chair, which will simply fold up when not in use. I love old folding military chairs, as they have a wonderful patina of age and wear in their structure and in the canvas fabric.

TOWELS, BATHROBES, AND MATS

After a good soak, wrapping yourself up in soft eco-towels is a must. Investigate organic fair-trade cotton towels, which will not contain chemical residues or have had a negative impact on the environment or on the communities that have grown the fabrics. Alternatively, you can look at pure linen towels, which will be absorbent but perhaps rather abrasive. Lastly, a great new alternative is towels made of bamboo fiber (woven onto an organic cotton backing sheet); they are wonderfully soft and fluffy and three times more absorbent than cotton, and their natural anti- bacterial quality stops them from getting moldy when damp. Due to bamboo's sustainable qualities and speed of growth, these are the towels of the future. Again, bathrobes and mats are available in a similar range of fabrics, from organic cottons to linen to bamboo.

CANDLES

The simplest mood lighting for a bathroom is the humble candle—its gentle flickering glow creates a warm, calm atmosphere. Seize the opportunity to add a touch of vintage by styling your bathroom with an ornate candelabra or chandelier (which could simply hang from the ceiling on a hook). In this unconventional setting, with its decorative detailing contrasted with the clean lines of the bathroom, it could look stunning—making a simple candlelit bath a romantic moment.

Be sure, though, to use natural soy- or palm-oil candles. If you choose scented candles, avoid artificial fragrances in favor of essential oils. These will not contain petrochemical products, which will release a black, sooty smoke known to contain toxins and carcinogens (see pages 89).

NATURAL SOAPS AND BATH OILS

There is now a wide variety of companies specializing in natural soaps and oils. On the whole, these will be better for sensitive skin, and are made with essential oils, and natural organic ingredients. By contrast, conventional bathing products can contain artificial scents, animal products, and petrochemicals, and can contain toxic parabens—not very relaxing when you start to think about it! Remember that the issue is not simply a matter of being kind to your skin but also a matter of how a product is made and what it does to the environment when it goes down the drain afterward.

MIRRORS

No bathroom is finished without the aid of a good mirror—essential for perfect grooming and making sure that you look your best before you leave in the morning. In a space that can all too often be dominated by technology and strong lines, it is worth considering a mirror that will restore some character to the space. Vintage or decorative mirrors can do this simply for you and will add extra richness to even the most humble of bathrooms. It is easy to track down old mirrors, but if you feel that they have too much detail or you do not like the ornate finish, you can paint the frame to match the wall color of your bathroom. This will help to tone down the overall effect, while adding a subtle opulence. If you prefer to buy a new mirror and want to choose one with a wooden frame, check that is made from FSC-sourced wood.

ABOVE This bathroom has a wonderfully wholesome feel. It balances technology (in modern faucets fitted with flow restrictors), nature (in the timber materials) and vintage (in the accessories). Now if only that lightbulb were changed to a low-energy version, it would be perfect!

BATHROOMS 123

BEDROOMS

WE SPEND MORE TIME IN THE BEDROOM THAN ANYWHERE ELSE (PROVIDED YOU LIKE A GOOD NIGHT'S SLEEP. . . IN YOUR OWN BED). A BEDROOM IS A SANCTUARY WHERE WE SLEEP, RELAX, AND READ. BEYOND THESE DREAMY PASTIMES, A BEDROOM SERVES A VARIETY OF PRACTICAL FUNCTIONS, INCLUDING STORAGE AND DRESSING. IT IS A SPACE TO RELAX IN AND A PLACE TO PREPARE FOR THE DAY AHEAD.

From an environmental perspective, the bedroom does not demand as obviously high a level of resources as either the kitchen or the bathroom. However, it is still a space that needs careful ecological thought when considering its decoration and furnishings. Of course, style plays an all-important role when planning a bedroom.

ABOVE A modern take on the four-poster bed in cool, natural-fiber bed linens, and an assortment of vintage furniture and antique objects all add up to the quintessential eco-chic bedroom.

The main steps that you need to take for an eco-conscious bedroom are to

● cut down on energy use, in the form of heating and lighting;

● minimize toxins in materials and finishes;

● reduce the levels of dust, which can lead to asthma and allergies;

🌿 Use organic fair-trade fabrics for all bed linens, thereby easing your eco-conscience for a really good night's sleep.

A bedroom being a space that requires few technological resources, its style relies more heavily on the use of the natural and the vintage. That said, as with any room in the house, making it environmentally efficient will also make it a more comfortable place to spend time in. So you will want to

● reduce any drafts that may result from badly fitting windows. If your windows are leaking cold air, fit roll caulking or foam strips. Alternatively, cover the windows on the inside with plastic film intended as a temporary substitute for storm windows; or fit real storm windows, or even double glazing.

● reduce heat loss from chimneys and fireplaces, either by boarding up the flue or by buying an inflatable balloon. When inflated, the balloon will fill the lower section of the flue, blocking drafts and stopping any soot from dropping down the chimney into the fireplace.

● retain a low level of ventilation within the room to prevent moisture and condensation levels from building up in the room and creating mould.

● create the right lighting levels, using low-energy lightbulbs, preferably LEDs.

● if you're away from home during the day, fit an automatic setback thermostat, which you can program to reduce the temperature while you're out and bring it up to a comfortable 68°F in the evening.

● if you have steam heat, you can fit thermostatic valves to your bedroom radiators to keep this room at the desired temperature.

🌿 insulate windows with thick draperies, which will also help to prevent heat radiating into the room during the summer. Make sure the draperies have a "return" to the wall at each side.

A greater grounding quality can be harnessed by using nature in the bedroom—textural materials that help to create a healthy space free of chemicals and toxins. A variety of natural materials can be used for bedroom furniture, floorings, wall surfaces, and, of course, fabrics.

The use of vintage items in the bedroom imparts an individual identity onto the space—after all, it is your private area, so make it unique to you, with treasured items that you enjoy and that say something about who you are. Personal collections and objects displayed in your bedroom will reflect you and your experiences, allowing you to relax into a space that suits you perfectly. Vintage items can also add a romantic quality, allowing you to revel in a sense of nostalgia about your life or shared experiences with your partner, be they mementoes of time spent together or pieces chosen in antique stores, markets, or on travels. Even in a bedroom, the softening effect of vintage pieces on the harder edges of a clean-cut contemporary space is useful. A worn leather armchair might be juxtaposed with a modern cabinet, for example, to set up an enticing visual contrast.

BEDS

As the most prominent piece of furniture in the room, your bed is its focal point. Beds are also the most well-used pieces of furniture in your entire home, so it is essential that you make the right choice. From an environmental point of view, you need to consider both aspects of your bed; the mattress and the frame itself.

Both the nature and vintage options offer sound environmental choices for beds. Natural wood frames supply a robust texture and warmth; however, they must carry FSC certification (see page 57). If not, they could have been made with illegally logged timber from an unsustainable source, such as virgin forest. Just how well would you sleep, knowing that your bed may have had a harmful and unnecessary impact on the environment?

Vintage bed frames have been popular for a number of years, as they lend an air of nostalgic romance, though they need not be overtly feminine. Search in antique shops and at auction houses or online auction sites.

Some typical vintage beds you may find are
❀ ornate wrought-iron beds—curvaceous metalwork adds a fairytale princess feel;
❀ classic paneled wood beds—solid, plain, and simple.
❀ decorative upholstered French-style beds—opulent and elegant, strong and yet romantic;
❀ four-poster beds—to give your bedroom an aura of colonial or antebellum charm;
❀ intricately carved wooden Art Deco-style beds—for a real vintage look;
❀ simple cast-iron bedsteads with vertical rails—they can be elegant, but also suit a

shabby-chic look. These are best stripped or sandblasted, to remove any possible traces of old lead paintwork, before being repainted.

Alternatively, construct your own bed frame; take pleasure in making something that you will use every day. That is not to say it must be expertly crafted, but if thoughtfully designed, a bed can speak volumes about the character of your most personal space. Previously I have constructed beds from wooden shipping pallets, a reclaimed shop display system (much like a small scaffold system), and lumber salvaged from film sets. Searching out the material adds to the excitement of creating something unique.

Currently my bed is made from a futon base with sides faced with reclaimed wooden floorboards to give it a soft, aged feel. The whole frame has concealed legs set back from the sides to convey the impression the bed is floating, rather like a magical flying carpet. To enhance this effect, the bed is underlit with a string of low-energy Christmas lights, which twinkle at night and enhance the sensation that the bed is hovering, ready to whisk me off to the mystical Land of Sleep.

If making your own bed frame, make sure the mattress will be properly supported by building in wooden slats with gaps of less than 2 in. between them. These slats can be attached to an existing frame or form the basis of a new frame. Keep an open mind when considering the bed's headboard and legs; both elements offer a chance to be creative. Because a bed is a mainly horizontal feature, any vertical element, such as the headboard, may really stand out. Consider the following sources when searching for materials for your bed frame:

RIGHT Technology, nature, and vintage are brought together here with a low-energy bulb being concealed within the decadent antique chandelier, contrasting wonderfully with the weathered lumber headboard. Organic cotton bedlinen, cushions, and soft woollen throws add a sensuality to this most personal of spaces.

❋ RECLAIMED LUMBER YARDS—for old doors, aged floorboards, disused pallets, gnarled pieces of wood, or turned newel posts from stairs. Take care not to use any materials that may have previously been coated in toxic preservatives such as creosote.

❋ CAR SCRAP HEAPS—for enormous shock-absorbing springs and many other odds and ends, perhaps even a retro car dashboard.

❋ SCRAP METAL YARDS—for all sorts of inspirational items, such as metal panels, scaffold parts, old signage, and trolleys with oversized wheels

❋ FLEA MARKETS—for antique bed frames that can be incorporated into new designs, vintage screens, reclaimed furniture that can be re-appropriated, vintage fabrics for coverings, and an amazing assortment of other pieces.

MATTRESSES

Considering the amount of time we spend lying on our mattresses, it is essential to choose one made with both health and comfort in mind. Conventional mattresses are treated with fire retardants and so contain residues of chemicals. Moreover, the growing of fibers and manufacturing of fabrics used in such mattresses incorporate toxins, including pesticides. An organic mattress or futon will benefit not just you but also the environment within which the materials were produced in the first place.

Constructed in a similar way to a conventional mattress, an organic mattress simply uses natural materials, such as wool and cotton, which are sourced from a carefully monitored chain of suppliers, none of which will have used the commonplace cocktail of chemicals in their production. What is more, they also reduce the need for harmful fire retardants by using non-combustible materials, such as wool.

A more expensive alternative to an organic mattress is a natural latex mattress. Tapped from rubber trees, latex has a unique elasticity and flexibility, allowing your body to be evenly supported. Considered hypoallergenic, these mattresses are free from animal hair and chemical additives and are resistant to dust mites, so are recommended for allergy sufferers or those with skin conditions. The latex is generally encased in an organic cotton removable sleeve, which can be washed, thereby further reducing the amount of dust buildup.

Because a latex mattress is warmer to sleep on than a conventional mattress, you will need only a thin quilt or duvet, so you can turn down the

heating in your bedroom; this kind of mattress is the perfect eco-solution, being better for you and reducing the energy consumed.

If you are not planning to change your mattress but are concerned about rising levels of allergies, then you may want to consider getting your mattress cleaned regularly. Over the course of the year your body will shed around 2 pounds of skin and 65 gallons of perspiration. Combined with the warm conditions in your bed, this makes it the ideal

ABOVE Use vintage to create an atmosphere that suits your home. In this case, the owners has given their bedroom a simple, yet romantic French feel.

breeding ground for dust mites; it is estimated that the average full-size mattress contains over 1 million mites. So although I know you don't really want to think about this, it is the dust mite droppings that are directly responsible for respiratory problems, such as asthma, and skin allergies, such as eczema. Every time you move around in your bed, these particles are likely to be inhaled.

If you are concerned—and you really should be—aim to reduce the number of dust mite droppings within your bed by vacuuming it thoroughly once a week. Alternatively, try to reduce the moisture content of your bed, which encourages the mites, by airing it on a daily basis—this is also a good excuse not to make your bed each morning.

There are also a number of naturally based sprays that can be used directly on the mattress to kill off the mites, after which they can be vacuumed up. This process will have to be regularly repeated so as to prevent continued buildup.

STORAGE

For a truly restful bedroom, you'll want not only a comfortable bed but enough storage space so that you can keep clutter out of sight. If you're lucky enough to have a spacious walk-in closet, this will be easy; but if you have only a reach-in closet, you may find that clothing, shoes, and other accessories are encroaching on your living space.

There are several possible solutions to this problem. Your existing closet may just need reorganizing and the addition of some new rods, shelves, or drawers. For example, an extra rod at waist level, under the existing rod, will give you twice the hanging space for jackets, pants, and shirts/blouses. To get some ideas, visit the Web sites of companies that make closet systems.

ADDING STORAGE

If the closet is simply too small for your needs, consider building a new one out into the bedroom. For a smooth, built-in effect, this could occupy a whole wall. Admittedly, this would take a large chunk out of your floor space—about 22 in. is required to accommodate the width of a typical garment—but if fitted with drawers and shelves as well as rods, it might enable you to get rid of some freestanding storage, such as a chest of drawers.

With large areas of flat board needed to construct a closet system—not to mention a whole new built-in closet—the choice of materials is crucial. If possible, choose solid lumber, such as pine or, even better, cedar—which will make your clothes smell great and keep moths and silverfish at bay. If you opt for plywood or MDF (medium-density fiberboard),

make sure it contains little or no formaldehyde, which is a known carcinogen. ZF (zero-formaldehyde)-MFD is more expensive than the ordinary kind, but a much safer option. Any lumber you use should be certified by the FSC. The same considerations apply, of course, to a purchased closet organizer system. And make sure that any paint used is a natural paint containing no VOCs, such as a water-based eggshell.

FREESTANDING STORAGE

If you haven't got enough floor space for a new built-in closet, there are some attractive options in freestanding furniture. Chief among these is the armoire. One of these will add instant old-fashioned, European-style charm to a bedroom. Vintage examples can be found in secondhand stores, antique shops, and online auction sites. They're generally not so efficiently designed as a custom-made closet system, but the larger ones can hold a surprising amount; you might fit one with some extra shelves to hold shoes or sweaters.

A chest of drawers is a virtual necessity if you don't have a really spacious and well organized closet. And a hope chest, placed at the bottom of the bed, can hold extra quilts or blankets or anything else that needs to be stowed away most of the time. Here, too, vintage pieces can add character to the bedroom. And the great thing about freestanding storage, unlike the built-in type, is that you can take it with you when you move.

OPPOSITE Re-appropriating old display cabinets from shops or haberdashers is a great way to show off any collection that you are proud of, and if that is clothing, then it makes finding an item even easier.

ABOVE Being the most private space in the home, a bedroom can be the perfect place to indulge a personal collection or private passion—from a library of art books to a series of framed butterflies.

OPPOSITE Make space for the things that are important to you; a bedroom is a very personal space and so it should reflect your passions, character, and even life history.

ADDITIONAL STORAGE

Once the bulk of your clothes and accessories are stored and out of sight, have some fun creating more unusual forms of storage for all those other odds and ends, such as books, jewelry, and photographs, that you will need to house in your bedroom. Keep your eyes open for anything that can be fixed to a wall or that will sit stably on the floor, or tabletop. Of course you can buy sets of floating shelves or display cabinets, but this is a chance to get creative:

🌼 aged lumber or floorboards used as shelves
🌼 wooden fruit boxes stacked or fixed to walls
🌼 wooden wine cases or metal biscuit boxes
🌼 vintage leather suitcases
🌼 ornate metal brackets to use with shelves
🌼 old wooden drawers piled up and fixed to one another—possible different sizes
🌼 old metal mesh cages—like old school shoe lockers

To give an old cabinet or bedside table a new lease on life, consider these options:

🍂 Simply sand the piece down and then repaint it, using natural VOC-free paints.
🌼 If the piece is covered in layers of paint, sand it down, removing uneven amounts of paint to give it a distressed look.
🌼 Paint the interior a vibrant, shocking color for a real burst of energy.
🍂 Paint a section in natural paints, and cover another flat section with a matching wallpaper (perfect if you have leftover sections of wallpaper from a feature wall—it will coordinate the room).
🌼 Give it a soft, reflective touch by re-covering the front in gold or silver leaf squares.
🍂 Stencil an oversized motif of feathers, leaves, or historic patterns onto the piece using natural paints—giving the effect of a piece of interior graffiti.
🌼 Use upholsterers' nails (smooth dome-headed nails) to create a series of dotted patterns—stylized flower or leaf motifs work well, as the light catches them.
🌼 Replace the door handles and legs with something more eclectic such as vintage glass handles, or reclaimed cast-iron dragons' feet from a claw-foot bathtub.
🌼 Use découpage sections of cut-out paper, (such as magazine pages) to cover the exterior, and then varnish to seal it.
🌼 Make it glow—under-light the piece with Christmas lights or a low-energy fluorescent strip light—it is fun to experiment.
🌼 Use chalkboard paint to create a surface you can write on (best done over a solid floor surface, to avoid chalk dust buildup).

FABRICS

Fabrics play an essential role in softening a bedroom, helping to make the space more enticing. Not only are fabrics sensuous and soft to the touch; they also absorb noise, reducing echoes and making a more relaxed acoustic environment. From a visual point of view, they add another layer to the design of your bedroom, providing accent colors, visual texture, and, importantly, a chance to create an easy-to-change seasonal look without any great effort, expense, or wastefulness. So for a long-lasting bedroom style, focus on neutral background colors for walls and floors and look to change the fabric accessories on a more regular basis.

WINDOW TREATMENTS

If you want to minimize the amount of fabric to cut dust levels (and therefore dust mites), choose a simple roller shade or, for a bit more style, a Roman shade. Either of these options uses just enough fabric to cover the window—although a Roman shade is generally lined, which will reduce heat loss or, in summer, overheating. Alternatively, consider wooden Venetian blinds or plantation shutters (made from FSC-certified lumber, of course), which allow you to control the daylight levels within the space.

There are now many organic and fair-trade versions of fabrics such as cotton, linen, and hemp that are suitable for decorating. The difference is that these fabrics will not have been grown using pesticides, nor will they have contributed to unfair working practices—which gives them a reduced environmental and social impact from the very outset (see pages 76–83). The benefit for you, apart from a reduced level of guilt, is that they also will not contain chemical residues that could put toxins into your bedroom.

An exciting alternative is to use vintage fabrics. For those who hate to sew or balk at the expense of handmade or even ready-made options, this is the perfect way to bring a little urban eco-chic into your home. Scour markets and secondhand stores or online auction sites for ready-made vintage curtains and draperies.

If chosen carefully, these will be well made pieces that are lined (adding extra insulation to your windows) and have heading tape sewn on. Make sure that you have a tape measure and know the length and width of the window that you plan to cover. If the draperies are too short, they will simply look wrong. If they're too long, you might just allow them to drape luxuriously on the floor, for a sense of drama or even decadence. For a neater effect, get them hemmed to just clear the floor (a relatively inexpensive job), or hem them yourself.

Choosing the right vintage fabric type will have an impact on the style of your bedroom, so you will want to think carefully about where you are going with this. Choose from a selection of the following fabrics that are likely to be available:

OPPOSITE The simplicity of this space shows off the variety of vintage fabrics to wonderful effect, whilst the antique bed adds a real sense of grandeur, making the overall feel luxurious rather than nostalgic.

❀ country florals and traditional chintzes—for old-fashioned, feminine delicacy

❀ patchwork fabrics—for rustic "granny chic"

❀ rich, silky damasks—for opulent grandeur

❀ delicate lacework—for soft, filtered light and a romantic feel

❀ oriental silk—for mysterious exoticism

❀ vintage 1950s—for refined sophistication

❀ retro 1960s or '70s—for naïve playfulness

❀ Solid-color velvets—for bold banks of color

❀ old wool blankets (picnic style or Army gray or khaki)—for utilitarian comfort

BED LINENS

Since bed linens are the fabrics closest to your skin while you sleep, it makes good sense to ensure that your bed linen is as natural as possible, rather than full of toxins, and is produced in an ethical way. (See pages 76–83 for information on organic fair-trade cotton and bamboo.) Personally, I sleep better knowing that the bed linen I use has been produced in a fair-trade manner—last thing at night, it is easier to doze off with a clear conscience.

OPPOSITE Don't be afraid to dye vintage fabrics— sometimes it is simply the color that is offputting. Better to give an item a new lease on life than to let it remain unused, plus the results are surprisingly satisfying.

BELOW Layer up plain white sheets with textural knits to add impact and warmth.

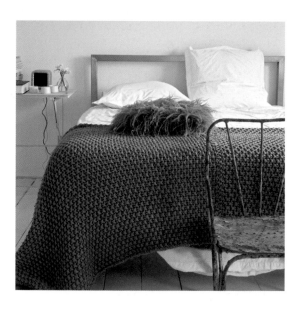

BEDCOVERS

Dressing a bed adds visual impact to the room and can make the bed look and feel sumptuous. A bedspread or throw can be surprisingly costly, particularly if you insist upon pure organic materials; however, you will feel the benefit. Natural fabrics, such as organic wool, cashmere, and alpaca, give a bed a warm, cozy feel that you just will not want to leave. A more cost-effective method of adding impact is to use a recycled wool blanket (possibly even made from recycled sweaters). Because of the small quantities of fabric used, these are produced in checked or plaid designs.

Alternatively, consider using vintage fabrics to dress your bed. Although covering it in swathes of fabric may be overkill, think about a gentle layering process by adding fabrics just to the foot of the bed. You may be lucky enough to find patchwork fabric throws. Why not consider making one, if your sewing skills are up to it? If the rest of the room is kept relatively free from decoration, strong color, and pattern, adding detailed vintage prints to a bed will work wonderfully. Updating vintage fabrics may just be a case of spending the time to dye them, so as to tie them in with the rest of your bedroom's color scheme. This can be carried out by hand or in the washing machine, but it is a good idea to check first that the fabric is natural (such as cotton or silk) and will take the dye.

Remember that using vintage pieces will add character and depth to this most personal of places—allowing you to suggest romance, history, and sophistication to your bedroom.

MIRRORS AND PICTURE FRAMES

Walls can be decorated with more than just natural paints, so consider embellishing them with mirrors and pictures. Mirrors will provide you with an opportunity to make yourself look your best before you step out of the house; but, of course, they also help to bounce light around your bedroom. Vintage mirrors will add depth and interest, their uneven reflective backing adding real depth and character to its appearance.

Being a private space, your bedroom walls can be used to display pictures of those you cherish. Although new frames are widely available, using an assortment of old frames will add individuality to every picture. To make the frames look more contemporary, think about unifying them by painting each frame the same color; this will highlight detail but make the differences subtler.

BEDROOM CHAIRS

If you have the luxury of space, adding a chair to your bedroom emphasizes the fact that this is a pleasurable space for spending leisure time in, rather than solely a place for sleeping in at night. Adding a place to sit gives the room an extra dimension—somewhere contemplation and perhaps conversation can happen.

Having said that, we do not all have the luxury of enough space for a languorous chaise longue; but you can instead use a small armchair or even a simple dining chair with arms. These can be dressed with cushions and throws to be made more inviting. If you are as messy as I am, the chair will become a clotheshorse at night—cutting out the need to fold and hang clothes back in the closet—a lazy person's temporary closet.

OPPOSITE Mirrors not only reflect views, they also help to bounce light back into spaces. In this case, the vintage bevelled-edged mirrors add a romantic essence to this bedroom.

RIGHT Positioned in a bedroom, a single chair can be "framed" by the space so invest in a chair that is a pleasure to look at—when it is not covered in clothes, that is.

CHILDREN'S BEDROOMS

FOR ANY PARENT, IT IS OF THE UTMOST IMPORTANCE THAT THEIR CHILD'S BEDROOM BE A SAFE SPACE FREE FROM TOXINS. BEYOND THAT, IT SHOULD BE A SPACE THAT IS FUN, INSPIRING, AND ORGANIZED. AND, OF COURSE, IT SHOULD NOT COMPROMISE OUR ECOSYSTEM.

FLOORS

To your child, the floor is a surface to crawl over, play on, and perhaps (given a child's ignorance of germs) even eat off. Because the child has so much contact with the floor, it is important to cut out dust and toxins, especially as a child's immune system is not fully developed.

● Carpets are soft and cushioning, but they trap dust and are breeding grounds for mites, increasing the risk of allergies and asthma. Do away with carpets to reduce dust levels.

● Artificial-fiber carpets contain high levels of toxins, such as stain inhibitors, fire retardants, and traces of pesticides. They will off-gas over time, especially when new.

● As an alternative to carpet, consider a rug (with an anti-slip mat) that can be readily cleaned and beaten outside to remove trapped dust. Buy one with a natural latex or burlap backing, as artificial latex contains toxins. Besides, if it gets damaged, it will cost less to replace.

● Alternatively opt for 100% natural pure wool carpet. Wool is the easiest of the natural-fiber carpets to clean and will not contain toxins in its upper or lower layers. Have it treated with a natural toxin-free stain inhibitor. Regular and thorough vacuum cleaning will also help to keep dust levels down.

● Solid floors reduce dust levels, because they are easier to clean. But stay away from floors that contain artificial materials, such as MDF, or layered floors using engineered wood. Instead, opt for a solid-material floor, such as solid lumber, cork (which has a natural spring to it), natural rubber, or linoleum.

● Avoid floorings stuck down with glues that off-gas formaldehyde as they dry. Specify natural nontoxic adhesives, such as natural latex.

FURNITURE

It is critical that you buy solid furniture. Not only is it likely to be harder wearing, but it will not contain toxins. Cheaper furniture is likely to be made from particleboard with a covering laminate of wood veneer, which uses a toxic formaldehyde glue to bond the wood particles together. Over time, this formaldehyde will off-gas into your child's sleeping area. Toxin-free solid wood should ideally be oiled, rather than finished with any VOC-containing varnishes or paints. If the retailer does not know whether an item is toxin free, simply do not take the risk.

BEDS

Your child's bed could be made from a steel frame or solid lumber; either will be hard-wearing and can eventually be recycled or sold on. Be aware that cheaper "wooden" beds are likely to made of laminates and so can off-gas toxins directly onto your child's pillow.

MATTRESSES AND BED LINENS

Mattresses are a source of toxic materials and in a very short time will harbor dust mites. So choose organic-fiber materials to make sure that no toxins (such as fertilizers, herbicides, fungicides, and pesticides) come into contact with your child's bed. You can now find mattresses that are made of natural organic materials, such as sheep's wool, natural latex, and coir, to ensure that the application of toxic fireproofing substances are unnecessary.

As your child gets older, consider a latex mattress with washable covers to inhibit dust mites. These latex mattresses are expensive, however; so if you do opt for a conventional mattress, vacuum it thoroughly every couple of weeks to keep dust mite levels down. Likewise, bed linen should come from an organic source. It is possible to buy fabrics, such as organic cotton and bamboo-fiber fabrics, that do not contain toxic chemical residues from their growth and processing (see pages 80–2).

TOYS

Throw out any vinyl toys. Vinyl is damaging in its fabrication, involving dangerous cocktails of chemicals. To make vinyl bendy, chemicals known as plasticizers are added. These have been shown to damage the liver, kidneys, lungs, and blood pressure, as well as the reproductive tract of boys. Since vinyl toys are often chewed, these toxins can be ingested. Instead, buy wooden toys, which are safe and will biodegrade.

OPPOSITE This child's bedroom does not have a single strong theme but rather pulls together lots of different fun natural and vintage elements.

RIGHT Vintage furniture will either have originally used a less toxic paint than modern equivalents or it will have had a chance to off-gas completely. This bureau offers space to work as well as the chance to display a collection of much-loved possessions.

LIVING ROOMS

THE LIVING ROOM IS THE KEY
SOCIAL SPACE IN YOUR HOME. IT IS
ALSO A PERSONAL ROOM, WHICH
CAN SPEAK VOLUMES ABOUT WHO
YOU ARE, THE INTERESTS YOU
HOLD, AND HOW YOU LIKE TO LIVE.
WHAT IS MORE, IT IS A MULTI-
FUNCTIONAL SPACE FOR RELAXING,
READING, WATCHING TELEVISION,
PLAYING, AND ENTERTAINING.

Living spaces often contain high levels of
technology, so it is important to reduce the
room's electrical loading as much as possible.
It is also crucial to recognize that all this
technology has a distinct visual impact on the
room. With cables, plugs, and an array of shiny
fascias, modern technology can lead to a high
level of clutter, which detracts from the focus of
the space. Our homes should embrace
technology, so that it is at the tips of our fingers
when we do need it but does not impact on our
lives when we do not. We need to find ways of
cleverly integrating—and perhaps even
concealing—technology wherever possible.

Creating the perfect urban eco-chic living room
relies on balancing our use of technology,
nature, and vintage, to make a space that is at
once efficient, comfortable, and characterful—
but the ultimate goal is to create a space that is
a pleasure to be in without impacting
unnecessarily on the environment.

ABOVE The living room of designer Lisa Whatmough is
peppered with her highly creative designs. She sources
neglected antiques, from armchairs to floor lamps, and

re-covers them in vintage fabrics. You may wonder how she gets so many different colors and patterns to work together; but somehow her artist's eye makes it happen.

ABOVE A log-burning stove is a far more efficient way of heating a space than an open fire. Furthermore, this stove creates a visual focal point to the living room giving it a rustic sense of warmth—and prevents ash and soot from spreading over the room.

FIREPLACES AND STOVES

A fireplace creates a focal point within a living room, around which you can position sofas, chairs, tables, and rugs. The flickering of real flames yields a restful quality; however, if you are intent on having an open fire, remember that up to 80% of the heat produced from conventional wood fires simply escapes up the chimney, so you cannot rely on it as part of a total heating system for your home.

A chimney acts as a funnel, designed to suck smoke up and out of your home. However, along with that smoke goes most of the heat produced by an open fire—or, if the chimney is unused, by your central heating system. Unused fireplaces can be capped to stop air movement – although this is by no means a simple task, as it involves accessing the uppermost part of your roof. Even so, you will still be heating the air inside the chimney breast. A better option is to seal the underside of the flue with a water-resistant plywood cover that prevents heat loss and dust from falling down the chimney. Alternatively, fit a chimney balloon inflated inside the lower part of the chimney, which prevents heat loss while retaining a low level of ventilation to the room.

A gas-fired, coal-effect fireplace has a similar level of heat loss, but with the added environmental downside of burning a carbon-heavy, non-renewable fuel. Consider instead a cast-iron or steel log-burning stove, which loses only around 20% of its heat up the chimney. For every four logs burned on an open fire, just one is needed in a wood-burning stove to create the same heat output. This means fewer logs to chop and less ash to clean. In addition, wood is a carbon-neutral fuel—it releases the same carbon when burned as it captures while it grows—so for conventional central heating, it is far less damaging to burn than gas. Added to the fact that wood is cheaper than gas in relation to the energy it creates, wood-burning stoves are an excellent option when considering your whole heating plan. On the downside, wood-burning stoves can be relatively expensive, so look online for secondhand models, or simply regard it as a sound home investment.

There is an enormous variety of stoves on the market. Many of them have glass fronts, so you can still enjoy the visual glow of a real fire but with the added advantages. It is essential to remember that with all wood-burning stoves, you will need a constant source of ventilation and a properly installed flue system.

If you have neither a conventional fireplace nor a hearth, an alternative may be a a flueless gel fireplace. A typical version consists of a steel box containing ceramic logs. It uses cans of nontoxic ethanol alcohol gel, derived from a biological source, such as corn or sugarcane, which comes in cans. This biofuel produces real flickering flames. The advantages are that you do not need a flue, which can let in drafts; 100% of the heat produced by the burners enters the room; and no ash is produced—giving you the visual impact of flickering flames without the downsides of a conventional fire. Because oxygen is still being burned it is important to ventilate the room properly. These units can be simply hung on a wall or worked into a conventional-looking fireplace. In either cases, they create a focal point for the room, diverting attention away from the television. Each can of gel burns for around three hours.

WINDOW TREATMENTS

With living rooms usually being sited on the ground floor, privacy may be an issue, so there is a balance to be struck between obscuring windows and maximizing the amount of natural light allowed to flood in. Although the normal rules on maximizing natural light apply (see pages 16 and 32) here are some stylish ideas for screening windows while allowing light in:

- sheer fabric Roman shades, left unlined to admit plenty of diffused light, venetian blinds made of FSC-certified wood, painted a light color or white
- Plantation shutters
- voile or sheer linen or muslin curtains
- translucent glass in lower window sections.
- translucent window film adhered to the panes
- translucent screens made from various materials, such as Japanese-inspired Shoji screens or even panels of thick tracing paper, weighted along the bottom edge.

LIGHTING

Often the main source of general, or ambient, light in a living room is a central pendant fixture. This should be fitted with a low-energy bulb. These bulbs are now dimmable, which makes their light variable and mood enhancing. Alternatively, make a grand lighting statement with a vintage chandelier; simply refit it with low-energy candle bulbs to marry the old and new. General lighting could also take the form of a spread of LED downlighters across the ceiling. Although intended as spotlights, LEDs will create a uniform spread of light when evenly spaced. Specify warm white LEDs, because standard LEDs are very blue, creating a cold feeling, which is inappropriate for living spaces.

Sidelights and table lamps create an intimate atmosphere. They can transform a space from a brightly lit, functional room into one of relaxed calm. Soft pools of light cast onto a side table or over the arm of a sofa entice you to sit and unwind. Low-level light alters the feel of the space, adding character. And because they are of a lower power, they can also help to reduce your overall electrical usage. Consider ways of introducing mood-enhancing lighting into your living room:

- low-energy LED spotlights directed onto pictures or architectural features
- ceiling-mounted colored LED downlighters, positioned to wash light down walls in soft scallop shapes
- strings of Christmas lights, wrapped around mirrors or picture frames, or piled in frosted vases or around logs in the fireplace
- LED color-changing table lights, producing soft, pulsing glows of differing shades
- rope lights coiled beneath pieces of furniture such as chairs or sideboards

OPPOSITE A variety of lights provide different levels of illumination to transform this room from a functional area (albeit lit by an opulent chandelier) into an intimate space cast in pools of light. Vintage light fittings are a great way to hide energy-saving bulbs and retain character.

FURNITURE

Furniture not only plays an important role in the style and comfort of your living room; it is also likely to represent a significant financial outlay. This is especially true of seating, which can be costly. Eco-friendly furniture, particularly sofas and armchairs, has been strangely slow in coming onto the market. Because this area of retail is so competitively priced, many retailers do not dare offer a sofa that is substantially more expensive, even if it does carry an environmental label.

Another barrier to furniture with a low environmental impact is that regulations state that upholstery must use fire retardants, many of which contain toxins. Although not every manufacturer uses all the following chemicals, some do. Be persistent in asking what any sofa contains, and be aware of the chemicals that may poison your body as you sit. Be aware that an inexpensive sofa is likely to contain

● brominated flame retardants—applied to upholstery fabrics and draperies, these hormone disruptors get stored long-term in the body
● phthalates—found in vinyl, these can be absorbed by the body and cause liver damage, reproductive and respiratory problems
● formaldehyde—found in plywood, carpets, and upholstery fabrics, this can cause nausea, headaches, rashes, and breathing difficulties
● volatile Organic Compounds (VOCs)—found in synthetic foams, these can affect breathing and increase the risk of allergies, cancers, and adverse neurological and reproductive effects.

Inexpensive leather sofas are a particular problem. Although they appear to be incredible value, they are upholstered in a fabric called bi-cast leather, which is formed by laminating very small pieces of leather onto a vinyl backing sheet. There are two problems with this method: firstly, the vinyl backing is likely to

OPPOSITE Simply designed, neutral-colored sofas have long-lasting appeal and can be seasonally redressed to suit, making it a more sustainable choice. The harder lines of this sofa are softened with feather-filled cushions and the use of decorative natural items on the table.

LEFT The carefully constructed patchwork-fabric covering of this elegant lounger gives it the welcoming feel of a much-loved "favorite armchair", and if it were to get damaged, well just add another patch. Making furniture easy to repair is important to sustainability.

contain phthalates, a known toxin listed above; secondly, although it looks like a nice leather sofa, it has no durability. A deep scratch or tear cannot be repaired, as it could on a sofa made of solid leather.

When choosing a sofa, the key is durability:
● Durability of materials—it should be solid and well made, with the wooden frame coming from a sustainable source. Removable covers give it extra life, as they can be easily be repaired or replaced when worn or damaged. Real leather softens and improves with age and is easy to clean.
● Durability of design—a simple, classic-design sofa will not go out of fashion quickly. Choose one in a neutral color and seasonally re-dress it with throws or cushions. If you choose a sofa in a bright color or heavy pattern, it is likely to age more quickly as your tastes and fashions change.

Alternatively, buy vintage or secondhand furniture; if it has contained toxins, it is more likely to have off-gassed already or may even predate the compulsory use of flame retardants in furniture. Particular favorites of mine are vintage leather sofas. A natural material, leather improves with age bringing a character to the home that is not precious, but warm and welcoming. Vintage furniture can be easy to live with, settling into your home more naturally and creating a softer overall feel. It is like the difference between your favorite pair of old jeans and a starchy new pair—some things are just better when they are a little worn. Otherwise, opt for a vintage fabric sofa and either have it entirely recovered or cover the removable cushions in several different fabrics for a relaxed mix-and-match look. If it has slipcovers, these can be cleaned, remade, or even dyed a darker color, for a low-cost transformation.

COFFEE TABLES AND SIDE TABLES

Smaller tables have the effect of softening the harder edges of other furniture in a living room; in front of a sofa, a coffee table provides a visual step down in height, as well as a surface for both decorative and functional objects. Side tables allow the convenient positioning of low-energy lamps. By helping to create a fore, middle, and background, small tables placed in the center of the room also have the unexpected visual effect of actually making the room feel bigger.

See tables as an additional opportunity to bring the urban eco-chic balance of technology, nature, and vintage into your living room. I find the idea of creating the perfect side or coffee table extremely exciting; being less purely functional than a chair, for example, these tables allow more scope for creativity. Be inspired by the following:

TECHNOLOGY

◉ Use a section of recycled plastic sheeting—mottled white surfaces will also help to reflect light into the room—and combine it with some vintage chrome table legs.

◉ Use a recycled glass surface—it may be expensive but it will be a real talking point. You could combine this with old wooden fruit boxes for a textural contrast. Views through the glass will show off the weathered boxes.

NATURE

🍂 If you are buying new wooden side tables, check that the wood comes from a sustainable, FSC-certified source.

🍂 Go to a lumberyard for a section of tree slice with the bark left on. Use a natural oil or wax to finish it and to bring out the texture of the grain.

VINTAGE

❀ Search flea markets, antique stores, or online, auction sites for antique or vintage tables—these will add a sense of sophisticated urban eco-chic to your home.

❀ Re-finish an old table by painting it, applying wallpaper to it, or even decorating it with mosaic tiles to cover the surface—this can be a relatively simple but exceptionally satisfying project.

OPPOSITE This charismatic living room relies heavily on the vintage to add character, which could be overpowering if weren't for the roughly hewn oak table, which adds a sensual yet contemporary feel.

LEFT The geometric lines of this natural wood floor offset the clean circular form of the table, and creating a contemporary Scandinavian aesthetic.

APPLIANCES

The modern living room is filled with technology, from stereos to televisions, DVD players, satellite boxes. and games consoles. This presents three problems. Firstly, your potential energy usage may be very high, so look for low-energy appliances and make sure they are all turned off when not in use. Secondly, this amount of technology leads to a lot of visual clutter from an array of shiny fascias, buttons, and plugs to miles of cabling. Lastly, where does it all go when it become obsolete?

It is all too easy to turn off the television from the remote control, but appliances left on standby can still use a wasteful 70% of the energy they consume when on. Make it a habit to turn everything off completely before leaving the room. If you've got several appliances in one area, plug them all into a plug-in outlet strip; you can then simply unplug the strip to turn off all the appliances at once.

The technology in your living room can detract from the relaxing, sociable atmosphere you're aiming for; it is a form of everyday visual pollution. Why not reveal the technology when you want to use it, but conceal when you do not. Look for specially designed cabinets that conceal televisions and all their associated technology. Alternatively, scour flea markets or online auction sites for vintage cabinets or small armoires that can be converted into technology cabinets by simply removing sections of the back to allow for ventilation or any elements of the television that extend outward. Depending on its style, this option may blend more seamlessly into your living space than a collection of electronic equipment. Or why not

consider adapting an existing cabinet to fit in with your home's decor. Paint it, wallpaper it, apply gold leaf to it, stencil it, or simply change the handles for a more personal effect.

As technology develops, television screens get ever bigger, become more difficult to conceal, and simultaneously use more energy. A recent report calculated that for the relative size of screen to the energy used, a video projector

onto a screen or a wall is the most efficient form of viewing. In my home, I have installed a video projection system with cables set into the wall from the set-top box to the projector. The speakers are concealed in the ceiling, and all electrical items are stored out of the way in a low-level plinth that runs the length of the room. This design highlights the fireplace and creates a seating area to either side of the hearth leaving the room free of clutter—while allowing for a whopping 5 ft. television screen when it is wanted.

The advancing pace of technology is frightening. As soon as you have read through the instruction booklet for your new television, the set is out of date. When upgrading, consider recycling the old appliances. Donate items to local charities, sell them on through online auction sites or local papers, or swap them via community sites.

ABOVE Combining technology with vintage can add another dimension to appliances. This television on its wheeled base need not be the permanent focal point of a living room—it can be wheeled away into a closet or corner.

THROWS AND BLANKETS

Throws really serve two purposes in your living room. First, they soften the harder lines of your furniture, making it look more inviting and helping to coordinate it with the space—think of them as a form of decorative layering that you can add to your living room. Secondly, and more environmentally, they will keep you warm as you curl up to read or watch TV. Being a place for sedentary activities, a living room would in theory require a slightly higher temperature than other rooms in the home. Resist the temptation to turn up the heat, and instead wrap yourself in a throw—thereby cutting your carbon emissions and lowering your heating bill.

A blanket or throw can also be made of an environmentally conscious material, which would have a reduced impact in its production and in terms of the chemicals that it might bring into your home. Think about using natural organic sheep's wool blankets—undyed preferably (available in creams, grays, and dark browns). An alternative—but with potentially a larger carbon footprint (and a higher price)— would be a wonderfully soft alpaca throw, created on small holding farms in South America (see page 81).

For a recycled fabric option, look into checked or plaid wool blankets made from reclaimed wool sweaters and scraps, although the tartan style look may not be to your taste. Alternatively, scour flea markets for old wool blankets or homely patchwork throws that may need just a good clean. If plaid and patchwork don't suit your decorating style, you might prefer my own favorite: old military blankets, which are available in gray or khaki from Army surplus stores. If they are pure wool and have been washed a number of times, they may have shrunk a little, which gives them extra thickness and a feltlike quality. I just cannot resist them and have stacks at home, perfect for winter evenings and hard-wearing enough for summer picnics and camping.

CUSHIONS

Adding cushions to your sofas and armchairs adds extra depth and warmth to their appearance—often, I think, a chair just is not quite complete without one. If chosen right, the color(s) of the cushion will offset that of the upholstery and will soften the harder lines of the furniture. Because their covers can be made of remnants, cushions are perfect objects for fabric recycling, and there is a plethora of such cushions on the market, providing the staple income of many a designer/maker. There are some beautiful cushions, and if you want to support local trade and creativity, it is worth checking out local art and design fairs or exhibitions for a unique piece.

Alternatively, why not try making some yourself. All you need is two squares of fabric, cut to fit a pillow form, plus a seam allowance. It's an easy little project, and a very satisfying one, made even better when friends come around and admire your handiwork. If you want a warm, familiar feel to your sofa, why not start by using your old unworn sweaters, sewing them up to fit a pillow form? If you are after something a little more professional looking, there are plenty of good materials to choose from, such as organic cotton, felt, and super-

soft alpaca. Some designers have really gone to town and made cushion covers out of hard-wearing factory waste, lengths of seatbelt webbing woven together, and even vintage shirts and ties. So there really is no end to the creativity that could be put into these pieces.

For a more relaxed, laid-back effect-which will also give you more flexible seating in your living room—buy or make some large floor cushions to place on a rug or carpet.

OPPOSITE These cushions and throws soften the stronger lines of the sofas, adding to their comfort and appeal.

ABOVE This well-worn leather armchair is given a final inviting touch with a soft, feather-filled cushion and wool throw.

WALL EMBELLISHMENTS

Seize the opportunity to add character to your walls; don't be limited to mirrors and framed pictures. Consider hanging objects that reflect your passions, whether they be antique fishing rods, vintage handbags, or your teenage record collection. Be inventive, and search out objects that tell the story of who you are. Look for early samplers, quirky examples of folk art, and unusual artifacts when you are travelling abroad. Collections of objects are perennially fascinating and add character to a space.

That said, framed photographs connect you to your family and past experiences, making a house feel more like a home. There is now an increasing range of picture frames made from reclaimed materials, such as teak, and byproducts of other industries, such as mango wood, bone, and mother of pearl, which would otherwise be discarded. These are often supplementary industries that spring up in developing countries, and they can help local communities become increasingly self-sufficient. Although many are uncertified, these industries often operate under fair-trade principles; but ask exactly what these are.

Of course you also have the vintage option; and there is wide availability of old picture frames at flea markets, secondhand stores, and antique shops. Coordinate them by painting them to match or to harmonize with your wall color.

OPPOSITE This room successfully blends the natural and vintage aspects of urban eco chic; the contemporary artwork gives this living room a vital modern edge, adding real vibrancy and energy.

PLANTS AND FLOWERS

Plants add an often much-needed burst of natural color to a living room. Displaying nature is a great way to stay in touch with the seasons, provided you do not buy flowers that have been air-freighted from overseas. Instead of high-impact imported blooms, consider displaying small branches of blossom, berries, and hand-picked flowers from your garden. Moreover, some plants can be very effective at soaking up toxins and CO_2 in the environment—while releasing oxygen. Plants such as Chinese evergreen, peace lilies, spider plants, aspidistra, lady palm, bamboo palms, Boston ferns, chrysanthemums, and gerberas are all excellent air purifiers. They will need varying degrees of light and water to live.

ECO-VASES

There is a good variety of recycled glass vases available, from everyday cylindrical ones to adventurous pieces. But a glass vase does not need to be big to display its eco-credentials. Dutch designer Tord Boontje, with his partner Emma Woofenden, has created a beautiful set of vases made from cut and frosted wine bottles. Manufactured by a Guatemalan cooperative aimed at getting artisans off the street and back into work, they are part of the Design with Conscience Campaign. Although not very big, they hold a simple stem or a few flowers.

Also available are quirky wooly knitted bottle vase covers. Simply drink your wine, wash the bottle, then slip the knitted cooler over the bottle's neck, and there you have it: an elegant inventive vase made from an item recycled from your meal—simply brilliant.

HOME OFFICE

OUR RELIANCE ON TECHNOLOGY TO CONNECT US TO THE WORLD HAS BROUGHT THE PERSONAL COMPUTER INTO THE HOME AND, WITH IT, THE HOME OFFICE. WHETHER ITS PURPOSE IS TO WORK FROM HOME, STAY IN CONTACT WITH FRIENDS, OR PLAY GAMES, THE HOME OFFICE LOOKS SET TO STAY.

A home office increases the pressure on your personal space but also offers environmental benefits. Not only does it allow you to work from home, thereby avoiding unnecessary journeys into the office, but it makes a whole tranche of information readily accessible, so that you can thoroughly research the key decisions you need to make in your life. Making informed choices helps to reduce your carbon footprint. In this way you can find local suppliers, research toxins, investigate sustainable alternatives, and make energy savings.

Your home office may be a dedicated room, shared room (perhaps also a guest room), or space in another room that is large enough to house all the necessary technology. Wherever you locate your office, make a positive effort to create a happy, healthy place to work; you will benefit from it physically, mentally, and creatively. Ventilate the space properly; make sure windows can be opened for fresh air. Plants bring vibrancy and energy, as well as helping to clean the air. Also consider using scented candles, which can create a calmer working environment.

But how can creating a balance between the principles of technology, nature, and vintage help you to create a better work space? Technology is key to the home office. It provides not just efficient energy-reducing machines and lighting but also better communication systems, which reduce your need to travel. It can also help you to cut down on resources, such as paper, by storing information rather than having to print it out. From a materials point of view, it can create a fresh, bright, and dust-reducing space that will be better for you and the technology that you are using.

OPPOSITE A home office space can be incorporated into any room and can be as simple as a trestle table, comfortable chairs, and adequate task lighting.

Nature has a grounding influence in the work space. The textural quality of natural materials will limit the buildup of the contributors to sick building syndrome, such as static electricity, and will help you to relax at work by reducing stress. Nature also helps to lower the level of toxins in the air through the use of VOC-free paints and plants, which make a space feel vibrant and more alive.

Vintage items can help you to feel relaxed, comfortable, and inspired. This is a great space in which to make small collections of objects that capture your imagination, no matter how different they are from your actual day-to-day work. Using vintage furniture in your home office, such as an antique desk chair or lamp, creates textural contrasts in the space, which will be more exciting and help to create a relaxed feeling—a world away from uptight corporate boardrooms with twenty identical chairs regimented around a large meeting table.

WALLS

Use pale shades throughout your work space to keep it feeling fresh and to bounce natural light around, but being an office you may also wish to paint the space either above or behind your desk with a vibrant energy-boosting colour. Natural paints are available in a wide range of colors, so it is now possible to find bold shades that will not bring toxic VOCs into your home. Take inspiration from the vibrant natural greens of spring or the warm autumnal shades of orange. You may want to pin up inspirational images or even spreadsheets on your walls; to do this, use recycled newspaper pulp board called Sundeala, which is strong but soft enough to take thumbtacks.

RIGHT Good storage adds real flexibility to the home office, allowing all your private papers to be quickly and neatly tidied away and leaving the room free to be used for other functions, such as a guest bedroom.

FURNITURE

If your home office is a shared space, flexibility is key. You may want to invest in a foldaway or sofa bed if using your spare bedroom, which allows you to maximize the office space when no guests are staying. Conversely, you may want to find ways of closing up your desk area when you do have guests, so they can relax without feeling as if they are prying into your affairs. A built-in work space with hinged or sliding doors could be the answer, but may require a cabinetmaker to construct it.

If your study is a limited area within a larger space, pack it away. Psychologically, this is important; when your working hours are over, your desk and anything unfinished remain out of sight. Transform an armoire into a study cabinet, creating something unique from an antique. Source sliding brackets and hinges from hardware stores. Make sure the heights of any surfaces are correct by copying the dimensions of an existing comfortable desk.

WORK DESKS

Depending on your office space, your desk size may vary greatly. If you have the luxury of a dedicated room, the desk could be of a standard size but made of different materials:
● **TECHNOLOGY**—use recycled plastic sheeting to create a sleek surface, fixing legs or trestles for a simple, industrial aesthetic.
🍂 **NATURE**—buy or make a wooden desk that uses FSC-certified lumber.
❀ **VINTAGE**—reclaim an old steel or wooden desk and make it your own. Strip steel down to the bare metal for a retro feel; a wooden desk can be stripped, stained, or painted.

DESK CHAIRS

It is a sad reality that one of the most common complaints of those working at home is the increase in repetitive strain injury (RSI). Using the right office chair, rather than simply any old kitchen chair, can combat this.

The office chair has moved on a long way recently; a number of manufacturers are taking seriously the issues of ergonomics and sustainability. Desk chairs are now fully flexible, with adjustments in seat height, armrests, and back support—creating a better, healthier seating position with total support for the spine. From a sustainability perspective, some office chairs are manufactured with a high recycled material content and are being designed with a minimal number of parts (which are easy to disassemble in as little as five minutes), up to 99% of which can then be recycled. It is now possible to choose a desk chair that is better for you, while also being beautiful and caring of the environment.

But a home office is not only a space for sitting at a desk, typing away. You may want to create a relaxed seating area as well, offering a quiet space to take a welcome break from the computer. The addition of a comfortable armchair goes a long way in creating a more welcoming work environment. Although you could look for some slouchy seating or even a beanbag, a vintage armchair will add a homely but textural element, contrasting with and softening the harder edges of a more dynamic, technology-filled workspace. If you have the space, it is a luxury well worth considering.

SHELVING AND STORAGE

Good storage is essential for a clutter-free work space, keeping what you need on hand but without visually polluting your office. You should consider immediate storage for pieces that you use every day, such as pens, pencils, paper; medium-term storage for occasional items, such as books and files; and long-term storage for anything used only every so often.

Storage can take the form of built-in shelves, cabinets, or freestanding units. In addition, make room for the display of those items that inspire you. It may seem whimsical, but these objects or collections are aides-mémoire, reminding you of who you are and your passions. They bring a touch of inspirational nature or vintage into your work space.

OPPOSITE Industrial metal shelving makes a stylish storage option for a home office, especially if you soften the harsh edges of the steel with your personal collections of books and memorabilia.

ABOVE A minimalist all-white office has been cleverly fitted into the corner of a spare room by using a shaped desk. The wall-mounted plastic storage board keeps everything in its place and the work surface uncluttered.

REDUCE AND RECYCLE

By using all that technology has to offer, you can create a more efficient workspace—one that uses less electricity and other resources, such as paper. As you work, make sure that you
● turn off all appliances when you finish for the day. In some cases, you may need to unplug them; check the instruction manual or your dealer;
● make the most of communication technologies, such as digital imaging; conference calling, and broadband, in order to reduce the need for travel and mailing items;
● use recycled paper in your printer;
● print on both sides of paper (though you may need a thicker grade of paper to do this);
● keep two wastebaskets—one for ordinary trash and one specifically for paper and envelopes—this also makes paper easier to reuse, provided you do not crush it up;
● recycle your empty printer cartridges—they are valuable to others;
● recycle obsolete items of I.T.—look online for charities that will take old computers and printers away for use in schools or developing countries or for local community groups, such as freecycle.org. If it is totally out of date, contact your local government, who can advise how best to dispose of any items without sending them to landfill.

OPPOSITE Plants can do a lot for the home office environment. The color and scent of a plant enliven the atmosphere of a work space, serving as a direct link to nature. Research has shown that plants can help to lower your blood pressure and stress levels, increase productivity, and remove airborne toxins that can leak from plastics, computers, and printers, as well as absorbing carbon dioxide and emitting oxygen—thus creating an enlivening and concentration-boosting breath of fresh air.

LIGHTING

Good lighting is key for a task-heavy area, such as a work space. While utilizing all available natural daylight to avoid using electrical lighting, you will need to reduce any glare from the sun and reflection on your screen, which can make computer work uncomfortable. So besides increasing the natural or reflected light into the space (see pages 16 and 32), you may also want to fit windows with solar shading devices. Consider shades or venetian blinds; the latter can easily be adjusted, depending on the time of day and angle of the sun.

For general lighting, aim for an even spread of light across the room. A consistent level of illumination makes a room safer to move around and eases eyestrain, since you do not have to focus from light to dark areas. A single pendant lamp or ceiling-mounted spotlights with low-energy bulbs may suffice, but it is likely your desk will be positioned against a wall, throwing shadows onto your desk and keyboard. A better solution is to install a spread of low-energy LED spotlights across the ceiling. This will give you an even array of general light, as well as direct task light over your desk area.

To create the right level of illumination on your desk, you may need an additional task light, such as a swingarm or other kind of desk lamp. Choose one with a shade sufficient to reduce the impact of any glare on your eyes and one that has a good level of built-in flexibility, making it as adjustable as possible. To give yourself maximum desk space, choose an adjustable floor lamp, such as a New York-style loft lamp. However, there is also a new generation of LED or low-energy fluorescent task lights available.

ENTRANCES AND HALLWAYS

ENTRANCES AND CONNECTING SPACES ARE OFTEN NEGLECTED, BUT OFFER A KEY OPPORTUNITY TO MAKE A HOME FEEL COHESIVE, VIBRANT, AND LOVED. MANY CULTURES REVERE THE HOME'S THRESHOLD—REGARDING IT AS A SYMBOL OF POWER AND WEALTH AND A SACRED SPACE—AND DECORATE ENTRANCES WITH ORNATE METALWORK, CARVINGS OR, FLOWERS.

BELOW It is possible to inject personality and humor into even the smallest of spaces. I love this quirky coat hook feature; it is both a functional and creative statement.

OPPOSITE Hallways serve more purposes than you may think, so multi-functional spaces like this add warmth and character whilst allowing you to get your coat and shoes on, and check yourself in the mirror, before leaving the house.

From even a basic, plain front door we make assumptions about the sort of people who live within that home. Going on first impressions, we can often surmise whether they are home-loving, D. I. Y. enthusiasts, have children, keep pets, prefer a tidy home, or live in organized chaos. First impressions do count, and if you want to convey a sense of who you are, this is the most public place in which to do it.

From a practical point of view, front doors and hallways act as a barrier and buffer to the environment beyond—providing security, light, and insulation from the cold or heat. It is also worth remembering that drafts account for on average 15% of the heat loss in our houses. As with any space in the home, we need to combine practicality, style, and environmental awareness to create a hallway that truly represents you as a follower of urban eco-chic.

A balance can be found between the use of technology, nature, and vintage in entrances and hallways. The use of technology adds warmth by means of insulation and draft exclusion in doors and windows, reducing your energy consumption. The careful use of glass—by adding a sky light, perhaps—will allow light to filter through into the space, reducing the need for electric lighting.

Using nature benefits hallways with hard-wearing materials that can withstand heavy traffic and at the same time demonstrate care for the environment. The use of vintage can impart identity and individuality to even the smallest space; and if you use an antique mirror, this will subtly bounce light around.

DOORS

Fitting a new door will improve your home security, cut drafts blowing through each room, and give the façade a facelift. A number of manufacturers can design, make, and fit a new front door in either traditional or contemporary styles. Make sure that any new door

- uses lumber from an FSC-certified source;
- uses sealed double-glazed panes for any glass;
- complies with all building codes;
- incorporates integral draft control;
- uses recyclable door furniture (stainless steel);
- uses locks that meet all required standards.

However, if you do not want a new or period-style front door, there is always the vintage option. Carefully note the key measurements of your door, then take a trip to your local reclamation yard; they are likely to have the door types prevalent in your area. Check for any warps or splits in the lumber and cracks in glass panels. If you cannot find a door that is an exact fit, buy one that is marginally larger, so it can be trimmed down. But go cautiously—take too much off, and you may ruin the structure of the woodwork. Because doors are heavy and need precise fitting, this may be best carried out by an experienced carpenter.

As a designer, I have a deep dislike of molded uPVC doors that imitate period styles. Although it can be strong and insulating, uPVC is a harmful material to create. It visually degrades as it ages, and it is nondegradable and difficult to recycle. On top of all this, to me these doors look cheap, and so I would always seek a wooden alternative and fit weather strips and covers to the locks and mail slot.

LIGHTING

Even when rooms are light and airy, the spaces that link them can feel dark and lifeless. If your house has a long hallway with no natural source of light, electric lighting will be called upon daily. To reduce your energy bills and CO_2 emissions, you have to work hard at finding ways to allow as much light as possible to filter into these spaces. Your efforts will be worth it; besides reducing your need for electricity, your hallways will come to life, feeling lighter and more vibrant. To keep your hallways light consider the following:

● Paint walls in light-reflective shades.
● Paint window frames and sills in light shades, so they bounce daylight straight in.
● Keep windows clean and unobstructed.
● Do not obscure windows with heavy draperies.
● Fit opaque or frosted glass panels into doors leading from rooms with windows.
● Fit roof lights or a solar light tube to bring light from the roof down to the hallway.
● Use toughened glass in balustrades and even stairs to filter light down from above.
● If your home has more than one floor, fit an upper level hallway with an opaque structural glass floor panel to filter light down.
● Fit automatic switches, limiting the time lights are left on. These can take the form of infrared movement detecting (PIR) switches which can activate lighting from just a few seconds to several minutes. They can also be adjusted to activate only once darkness falls.
🍂 Use light-reflective flooring, such as wood or ceramic tiles.
🌼 Hang vintage mirrors on hallway walls to bounce light in and through the space.

STORAGE

With the increasing demands on our homes to incorporate more and more functions, it is sometimes difficult to keep our homes and hallways clear of clutter. But a home with blocked passageways will exert an unseen yet suffocating pressure on your life. Squeezing past toys, recycling boxes, and even bikes will make entering, leaving, and moving around your home a hassle. It is up to you to put in place a system that makes your hallway a tidy, fluid space—one that is a pleasure to use and that says a little about who you are to visitors entering for the first time. Here are some practical considerations to keep in mind:

● Find a space, be it a table or hook, that you can put your keys on. Keep it out of sight of the front door to discourage burglars from reaching in and lifting them.
● Use bulldog clips screwed to the wall to hold mail and keep tabletops clear.
● Find spaces for recycling boxes, such as under the stairs, or build racks for them so they stack neatly out the way.
● Fix a hook on the back of your front door and hang a reusable shopping bag there, so that you will remember it whenever you leave home.
● Ban all toys from the hallway.
● Hang your bike by a wall or ceiling hook, if you must have it inside, so at least it is out the way and will not fall over.
● Make the most of all concealed "Cinderella spaces" for storing boxes or other bulky items. If the space under the stairs has not been touched for six months, clear it out and use it for storing items you use on a daily and weekly basis, like recycling boxes.

ABOVE A successful balance of the urban eco-chic principles of technology, nature, and vintage has been created here with the multi-striped stair runner, the rustic wooden table, and the vintage telephone. The result: a fresh, harmonious feel.

ECO RESOURCES

ECO INFORMATION

DATABASE OF STATE INCENTIVES FOR RENEWABLES AND EFFICIENCY
dsireusa.org
information on incentives for saving energy

FAIR TRADE CERTIFIED
transfairusa.org
information on Fair Trade programs and products

FRIENDS OF THE EARTH
foe.org
campaigns for a healthy environment

THE GREEN GUIDE
thegreenguide.com
National Geographic-sponsored web site offering advice on green living

U.S. DEPARTMENT OF ENERGY
eere.energy.gov
information on heating, cooling, insulation, electricity, and other "green" issues

RECYCLING SERVICES

DUMP AND RUN INC.
dumpandrun.org
organizes sales of college students' unwanted furniture and other belongings for charity

MY GREEN ELECTRONICS
mygreenelectronics.org
finds local corporate recycling schemes for electronic equipment

ECO HOMES

HEALTHY HOME PLANS
healthyhomeplans.com
architects' designs for eco-friendly living

LIVE GREEN, LIVE SMART
livegreenlivesmart.org
builders of the model "Sustainable House" and sponsors of the "50,000 Green Homes Initiative"

ENERGY EFFICIENCY

ELECTRONIC EDUCATIONAL DEVICES, INC.
wattsupmeters.com
Watts up? electricity meters

ENERGY STAR
energystar.gov
information on energy-efficient appliances and home improvements, including tax credits

HEATING/COOLING SYSTEMS

BIOMASS COMBUSTION SYSTEMS, INC.
biomasscombustion.com
biomass furnaces

FAHRENHEIT TECHNOLOGIES, INC.
fahrenheittech.com
biomass furnaces

PROGRAMMABLE THERMOSTATS
honeywell-thermostats.com
programmable thermostats

RADIANT HEATING.COM
radiantheating.com
radiant (infloor) heating/cooling systems

SOLAR SMART WATER HEATING SYSTEMS

solardepot.com
designs and supplies solar energy systems

TANKLESS WATER HEATERS

tankless-water-heater.com
importers of Stiebel Eltron and Takagi tankless heaters

WHOLE HOUSE FANS

wholehousefan.com
attic-mounted fans to reduce/eliminate the need for air-conditioning

ECO BUILDING MATERIALS

COLUMBIA FOREST PRODUCTS
columbiaforestproducts.com
manufacturers of formaldehyde-free hardwood plywood and hardwood veneer

DRI COMPANIES
dricompanies.com
T 949 266 3855
for Lumeta solar roof tiles

FOREST STEWARDSHIP COUNCIL
fscus.org
organization to promote the responsible management of the world's forests

TOOLBASE SERVICES
toolbase.org
information resource aimed primarily at building contractors; includes information on storm windows, recycled wood flooring, graywater systems, etc., and lists of manufacturers

ECO FLOORS

ARMSTRONG
armstrong.com
T 717 397 0611
linoleum and other floor coverings

COUNTRY FLOORS
countryfloors.com
stone, mosaic, terra cotta, ceramic tiles

ECO BY DESIGN
ecobydesign.com
T 626 969 3707
pure wool carpet, cork flooring, organic cotton rugs, other eco-friendly furnishings

PLYBOO (SMITH & FONG)
plyboo.com
T 866 835 9859
bamboo flooring; also end-grain bamboo chopping blocks

RUBBER-CAL
rubbercal.com
T 800 370 9152
rubber flooring and mats

SISAL CARPET.COM
sisalcarpet.com
T 877 757 4725
sisal and wool carpets

U.S. RUBBER RECYCLING, INC.
usrubber.com
T 909 825 1200
heavy-duty carpet tiles and other floorings made from recycled bus and truck tires

ECO WINDOWS

ALLIED WINDOW, INC.
alliedwindow.com
T 800 445 5411
"invisible" storm windows

BUY PLANTATION SHUTTERS
buyplantationshutters.com
T 800 823 6677
*plantation shutters; also
bamboo blinds*

SHENANDOAH SHUTTERS
shenandoahshutters.com
T 800 733 1549
all-wood plantation shutters

ECO WALLS

OLD VILLAGE PAINT
old-village.com
T 800 498 7687
*buttermilk paints and other
natural wall coverings*

**THE OLD FASHIONED
MILK PAINT CO., INC.**
milkpaint.com
T 866 350 6455
safe historic paints

ECO SURFACES

CORIAN
www2.dupont.com
*surfaces and sinks for
kitchens and bathrooms*

**ENDURA WOOD
PRODUCTS**
endurawood.com
T 503 233 7090
*countertops in sustainable,
reclaimed, recycled lumber*

PAPERSTONE
paperstoneproducts.com
T 360 538 9815
*recycled FSC-certified
paper in a resin base,
suitable for countertops*

3-FORM
3-form.com
T 800 726 0126
Varia (ecoresin) resin panels

VETRAZZO
vetrazzo.com
T 510 234 5550
*countertops of crushed
recycled glass set in cement*

ECO LIGHTING

ELIGHTS
elights.com
T 888 844 3332
*light fixtures, including low-
voltage outdoor lighting*

LIGHT BULBS ETC., INC.
lightbulbsdirect.com
T 888 757 9591
low-voltage lightbulbs

REJUVENATION
rejuvenation.com
T 888 401 1900
*eco-friendly direct marketer
of authentic reproduction
light fixtures*

SEA GULL LIGHTING
seagulllighting.com
T 800 347 5483
*low-voltage linear, track, and
rail lighting; also fixtures*

ECO KITCHENS

AGA
aga-ranges.com
*ranges made from 70%
recycled cast iron*

HGTV KITCHEN DESIGN
design.hgtv.com/kitchen
*video reports providing
guidance on designing your
own green kitchen*

NEIL KELLY CABINETS
neilkellycabinets.com
T 503 335 9207
*kitchen cabinets, made
from FSC-certified wood*

SUN FROST
sunfrost.com
T 707 822 9095
*highly energy-efficient
refrigerators and freezers*

VIKING
vikingrange.com
T 888 845 4641
*kitchen appliances including
glass ceramic induction
cooktops*

ECO BATHROOMS

CAROMA
caromausa.com
*dual-flush toilets and other
bathroom fixtures*

GROHE
groheamerica.com
T 630 582 7711
*water-saving faucets and
shower systems*

WATERCHECK.BIZ
watercheck.biz
T 888 222 0840
*various water-connected
products, including water-
conserving showerheads*

ECO FURNITURE

**COZYPURE ORGANIC
MATTRESS & BEDDING
COMPANY**
cozypure.com
T 800 229 7571
*natural latex mattresses,
organic cotton and wool bed
linens; wood platform beds*

**ENGINEERED PLASTIC
SYSTEMS LLC**
epsplasticlumber.com
T 847 289 8383
*furniture for house and
garden from recycled plastic*

RUBY LANE
search.rubylane.com/
antiques
armoires and wardrobes

SOLID WOOD CLOSETS
solidwoodclosets.com
T 800 351 9144
*formaldehyde-free solid
wood organizing systems
for walk-in closets*

**SUSIE JANE ORGANICS,
INC.**
susiejane.com
*eco-friendly furnishings for
babies and toddlers*

**VERMONT WOODS
STUDIOS**
vermontwoodsstudios.com
T 888 390 5571
*high-quality furniture from
sustainable sources and
reclaimed barnwood*

ECO FABRICS

ENVIRO TEXTILE.COM
envirotextile.com
T 970 945 5986
*manufacturers and
importers of hemp fabrics,
including fabrics suitable for
decorating and upholstery*

FACTORY DIRECT DRAPES
factorydirectdrapes.com
T 866 713 7273
*draperies, curtains, and
valances from organic
cotton*

HEART OF VERMONT
heartofvermont.com
T 800 639 4123
*pure wool and organic
cotton mattresses, futons,
and bed linens*

PICTURE CREDITS

The publisher has made every effort to trace the copyright holders. We apologize in advance for any unintentional omission and would be pleased to insert the appropriate acknowledgment in any subsequent edition.

2 Pernille Howalt/House of Pictures/styling Pernille Lykke; 9 Paul Massey/Living etc/IPC+ Syndication; 10–11 Istock; 12 Lars Ranek; 15 Marie Claire Maison/Mai-Linh/Box Managment/C.ARDOUIN/stylist Roxane BEIS home; 19 Simon Scarboro/stylist Maxine Brady; 22–3 Sharyn Cairns/Tuckey House; 24–5 Axolotl Group; 27 Ray Main/Mainstreamimages/ Oliver Heath Design; 39 Ray Main/Mainstreamimages; 42 Sharyn Cairns/Tuckey House; 44–5 Formica; 46 Louise Body Wallprint; 50–1 Ray Main/Mainstreamimages/Oliver Heath Design; 53 above left Ray Main/Mainstreamimages/ Oliver Heath Design; 53 above right Bamboo Flooring Company; 53 center left Dalsouple/Deacons Law Consultancy, Australia/photographer Robert Frith; 53 center right siestacorktiles.co.uk; 53 below left Hemp Fabric UK; 53 below right siestacorktiles.co.uk; 55 Mikkel Strange/Linnea Press/styling Jesper Grand; 56 Ray Main/Mainstreamimages; 59 © Narratives/Polly Wreford; 60 left Andreas von Einsiedel/interior design by Clare Lattin and Mark Hix; 60 right Henry Wilson/Redcover.com; 63 above left Martine Hamilton Knight/arcaid.co.uk; 63 above right Tom Leighton/Living etc/ IPC+ Syndication; 63 center left © 2005. All rights reserved. Image provided courtesy of 3form, Inc; 63 center right Louise Body Wallprint; 63 below left 100% recycled glass by Eluna; 63 below right Ed Reeve/Redcover.com; 64–5 Jens Stoltze/Linnea Press/styling Sidsel Zachariasen; 67 Marie Claire Maison/E.BARBE/C.ARDOUIN/by two architects: W.FEYFERLIK&S.FRITZER; 68 Marie Claire Maison/V.LEROUX/Temps Machine/C.ARDOUIN/stylist Marthe DESMOULINS home; 71 above right marcusbleyl.com/greenhouseeffect.co.uk; 71 above left Nathalie Krag/Taverne Agency/styled and produced by Tami Christiansen; 71 center left Ray Main/Mainstreamimages/Oliver Heath Design; 71 center right Istock; 71 below left photo courtesy of Smith & Fong Plyboo; 71 below right Gary Nicholson—Eight Inch Ltd; 73 above Ray Main/Mainstreamimages/Oliver Heath Design; 73 below Gary Nicholson—Eight Inch Ltd; 74 Ray Main/Mainstreamimages/David Gill; 77 above right Ray Main/Mainstreamimages/Oliver Heath Design; 77 above left Annie Sherburne; 77 center right © EcoCentric; 77 center left Ray Main/Mainstreamimages/squintlimited.com; 77 below left Marie Claire Maison/Mai-Linh/Box Managment/C.ARDOUIN/Anja&Parry KOOPS home, Balthazar Keuken, Amsterdam; 77 below right © EcoCentric; 79 Nathalie Krag/Taverne Agency/styled and produced by Tami Christiansen; 80 Winfried Heinze/Redcover.com; 83 above Henry Wilson/Redcover.com; 83 below Paul Massey/ Mainstreamimages; 85 above left OXO International and Phillips Provan International as the exclusive distributors; 85 above right Madeleine Boulesteix; 85 center left Ray Main/Mainstreamimages/Oliver Heath Design; 85 center right © Hotze Eisma; 85 below left Marie Claire Idées/L.GAILLARD/P.CHASTRES/A.CHATILLON; 85 below right re-foundobjects.com; 87 Mel Yates/Media 10 Images; 88 Lisbett Wedendahl/House of Pictures; 90–1 Istock; 92 Nathalie Krag/Taverne Agency/producer Tami Christiansen; 94 left Marie Claire Maison/V.LEROUX/ Temps Machine/C.ARDOUIN; 94 right Lars Ranek; 95 Marie Claire Maison/Mai-Linh/Box Managment/C.ARDOUIN; 98 Lars Ranek; 97 Marie Claire Maison/V.LEROUX/Temps Machine; 102 Mikkel Strange/Linnea Press/styling Jesper Grand; 104–5 Marie Claire Maison/V.LEROUX/Temps Machine/C.ARDOUIN/Stylist Marthe DESMOULINS home; 107 © Jefferson Smith/Sarah Wigglesworth Architects; 108 Lars Ranek; 111 Mikkel Adsbøl/Linnea Press/styling Pernille Vest; 112 Bieke Claessens/Redcover.com; 115 Mikkel Vang/Taverne Agency/production Christine Rudolph; 116 left Earl Carter/Taverne Agency/producer Anne Marie Kiely; 116 right Ray Main/Mainstreamimages/Foundassociates.com; 118 Mike Huibregtse, Manager—Photographic Art, Kohler Co; 119 Mike Huibregtse, Manager—Photographic Art, Kohler Co; 120 Bieke Claessens/Redcover.com; 123 Paul Massey/Living etc/IPC+ Syndication; 124 Paul Massey/Living etc/IPC+ Syndication; 127 Ray Main/Mainstreamimages/Oliver Heath Design; 128–9 Ray Main/Mainstreamimages/Jura Distillery; 131 Richard Birch/Living etc/IPC+ Syndication; 132 Marie Claire Maison/V.LEROUX/Temps Machine/C.ARDOUIN/Stylist Marthe DESMOULINS home; 133 Chris Tubbs/Media 10 Images; 135 Debi Treloar/Redcover.com; 136 Hotze Eisma/Taverne Agency/producer Julia Bird; 137 Marie Claire Maison/Mai-Linh/Box Managment/C.ARDOUIN/ Anja&Parry KOOPS home, Balthazar Keuken, Amsterdam; 138 Alun Callender/Redcover.com; 139 Ray Main/Mainstreamimages/designer Ben De Lisi; 141 Heidi Lerkenfeldt/Linnea Press/styling Pernille Vest; 142 Heidi Lerkenfeldt/Linnea Press/styling Pernille Vest; 143 Heidi Lerkenfeldt/Linnea Press/styling Pernille Vest; 144–5 Ray Main/ Mainstreamimages/squintlimited.com; 146 Edina van der Wyck/Media 10 Images; 148 Elizabeth Whiting Associates; 149 Andreas von Einsiedel/interior design by Clare Lattin and Mark Hix; 150 Hotze Eisma/Taverne Agency/producer Julia Bird; 151 Ray Main/Mainstreamimages/squintlimited.com; 152 Graham Atkins Hughes/Redcover.com; 153 Mikkel Adsbøl/Linnea Press/styling Hanne Vind; 154–5 Pernille Howalt/House of Pictures/styling Pernille Lykke; 156 Prue Ruscoe/Taverne Agency/producer Tami Christiansen; 157 Verity Welstead/Redcover.com; 159 Mikkel Adsbøl/Linnea Press/styling Hanne Vind; 161 Marie Claire Maison/Mai-Linh/Box Managment/C.ARDOUIN/Anja&Parry KOOPS home, Balthazar Keuken, Amsterdam; 162 Mikkel Adsbøl/Linnea Press/styling Hanne Vind; 164 Marie Claire Maison/ E.BARBE/C.ARDOUIN; 165 Lars Ranek; 166 Mikkel Adsbøl/Linnea Press/styling Hanne Vind; 168 Mikkel Adsbøl/Linnea Press/styling Hanne Vind; 169 Debi Treloar/Redcover.com; 171 Verity Welstead/Living etc/IPC+ Syndication.

The statistics quoted on pages 29–31 were provided by The Energy Saving Trust/energysavingtrust.org.uk.

INDEX

Figures in *italics* refer to captions.

ACKNOWLEDGEMENTS

I would like to thank all those people who have given me their time, expertise, and help in writing this book. To Nikki Blustin and Sarah Kahn at Blustin Heath Design for their research assistance, suggestions, and proofreading. To the team at EcoCentric—Michael, Niki, and Leena, who have spent so much time researching products and building the online store, which has influenced my thinking about Urban Eco Chic. Thank you, too, for all those that gave their time to help me in my research: Madeleine Boulestix, who makes such beautiful reclaimed chandeliers; Greta Corke, John Sawdon Smith, and Richard Woods at DIY Kyoto who design the most stylish of energy meters; Barley Massey and her wonderful recycled fabric; Jimmie Karlsson and Martin Nihlmar at Jimmie Martin who make their Baroque and Roll furniture; Piet Hein Eek, the most stylish reclaimed timber furniture designer ever; Gary Nicholson, who creates sparkling recycled glass work surfaces at Eight Inch; and Lisa Whatmough, whose patchwork chic furniture at Squint is such an inspiration. And last but not least for all those at my wonderful publishers, Quadrille, who have listened to my ideas and given them so much well-considered attention. In particular, thank you Jane, Helen, Lisa, and Claire.